The rise and rise of road transport, 1700–1990

Prepared for the Economic History Society by

Theo Barker
and
Dorian Gerhold

CAMBRIDGE
UNIVERSITY PRESS

Published by the Press Syndicate of the University of Cambridge
The Pitt Building, Trumpington Street, Cambridge CB2 1RP
40 West 20th Street, New York, NY 10011-4211, USA
10 Stamford Road, Oakleigh, Melbourne 3166, Australia

The Rise and Rise of Road Transport, 1700–1990 first published by
The Macmillan Press Limited 1993
First Cambridge University Press edition 1995

Printed in Great Britain at the University Press, Cambridge

A catalogue record for this book is available from the British Library

Library of Congress cataloguing in publication data applied for

ISBN 0 521 55280 X hardback
ISBN 0 521 55773 9 paperback

CE

The rise and rise of road transport, 1700–1990

┐

New Studies in Economic and Social History

Edited for the Economic History Society by
Michael Sanderson
University of East Anglia, Norwich

This series, specially commissioned by the Economic History Society, provides a guide to the current interpretations of the key themes of economic and social history in which advances have recently been made or in which there has been significant debate.

In recent times economic and social history has been one of the most flourishing areas of historical study. This has mirrored the increasing relevance of the economic and social sciences both in a student's choice of career and in forming a society at large more aware of the importance of these issues in their everyday lives. Moreover specialist interests in business, agricultural and welfare history, for example, have themselves burgeoned and there has been an increased interest in the economic development of the wider world. Stimulating as these scholarly developments have been for the specialist, the rapid advance of the subject and the quantity of new publications make it difficult for the reader to gain an overview of particular topics, let alone the whole field.

New Studies in Economic and Social History is intended for students and their teachers. It is designed to introduce them to fresh topics and to enable them to keep abreast of recent writing and debates. All the books in the series are written by a recognised authority in the subject, and the arguments and issues are set out in a critical but unpartisan fashion. The aim of the series is to survey the current state of scholarship, rather than to provide a set of prepackaged conclusions.

The series has been edited since its inception in 1968 by Professors M. W. Flinn, T. C. Smout and L. A. Clarkson, and is currently edited by Dr Michael Sanderson. From 1968 it was published by Macmillan as *Studies in Economic History*, and after 1974 as *Studies in Economic and Social History*. From 1995 *New Studies in Economic and Social History* is being published on behalf of the Economic History Society by Cambridge University Press. This new series includes some of the titles previously published by Macmillan as well as new titles, and reflects the ongoing development throughout the world of this rich seam of history.

For a full list of titles in print, please see the end of the book.

Contents

Tables

Introduction

Historians' neglect of road transport

Until recently the growth of Britain's road transport has been relatively neglected by historians. Even the attention it *did* receive was largely concentrated on turnpikes, road building and the improvement of road surfaces rather than upon what really mattered: the growing volume of traffic of various sorts which travelled along the roads. Part of the problem has been the relative scarcity of historical evidence, especially in comparison with canals and railways. Turnpike trusts have left plenty of records, but they rarely provide much information about traffic, and are often uninformative even about how the trusts improved their roads. Moreover, whereas a new canal or railway was an obvious physical development which often gave rise to identifiable changes in patterns of transport and economic activity, this was rarely the case with road improvements. Again, canals and railways, even when no longer in use, have left more visible evidence than roads and road services; and the peace of the canal towpath and the excitement of steam have attracted enthusiasts and given rise to societies and periodicals which have fostered research and a flood of publications. Road transport, by contrast, attracts few devotees and is associated all too often nowadays with frustrating traffic jams, dangerous pollution and deadly accidents.

The problem of sources has also affected the study of internal trade in general. Chartres showed in an earlier contribution to this series, *Internal Trade in England, 1500–1700* (1977), that overseas trade had received more than its fair share of attention from historians because it was recorded by customs officials, even though the poorly documented (and therefore less studied) inland trade in fact involved much greater volumes of goods. We shall argue that road transport in particular has been underestimated for much of its history. Underestimation applies to periods both before and after our starting date of 1700, for even as early as the fifteenth century there is evidence of considerable traffic by wheeled vehicle. Olive Coleman used the brokage books of Southampton to show that carts were heading in most directions from that port in 1443–4, with no fewer than 535 journeys being made to London alone in that year,[1] and Harrison has demonstrated the large number and high quality of the bridges existing as early as 1530, the great majority of them being wide enough for carts (D. F. Harrison).

There has been general agreement that road transport improved in the half century or so before the coming of railways; but even in that period it is the increasingly fast and frequent stage coaches with their relays of horses which have caught the attention of historians, rather than the less spectacular and ungainly stage waggons and the great variety and quantity of goods they carried. Before that period it has often been assumed that the roads were in so bad a state that road transport was necessarily unreliable and expensive. The most influential view was for a long time that of the Webbs. They argued not only that the parish roads were ill-maintained because of their dependence on ineffective statute labour, but also that turnpike roads, created piecemeal from the late seventeenth century onwards, formed an unsatisfactory system which was of limited value to through traffic, since stretches of turnpike were separated by miles of unimproved track: 'It took, in fact, practically a whole century of disconnected effort before even such national arteries of communication as the Great North Road from London to Edinburgh, the Irish road from London to Holyhead, or the Great Western Road from London to Exeter came, for the whole of their lengths, under the administration of Turnpike Trusts' (S. & B. Webb, *125*).

Other scholars, it is true, were less emphatic. Jackman, who made the most extensive study of both the printed and manuscript sources for his massive work published in 1916, realised that not all contemporary comment on England's roads was unfavourable, even before 1750. On the question of whether the roads were good or bad, he concluded that 'amidst the mass of conflicting testimony, it is extremely difficult to obtain a satisfactory answer to this question' (Jackman, 85). He also provided much evidence on road transport services and the ways they improved, such as the increased speed of coaches between 1750 and 1830. The several works on inland transport which appeared between 1959 and 1974 also stressed the improvement in road transport after about 1750 (Barker & Savage; Dyos & Aldcroft; Bagwell).

There was no denying, however, the much higher cost of road transport compared with water transport, and from this it was a short step to assigning to road transport an inferior role. As Dyos and Aldcroft put it in 1969, 'the chief highway of the English during the turnpike era was not the road at all but navigable water' (85). Mathias, in *The First Industrial Nation* (1983 edn), concurred: 'However good the road system, given the economics of freight transport by horse and wagon, the canals were the only medium which could sustain the impact of industrialization and urbanization before the railways', although he added that 'speed and regularity perhaps counted for more in the calculations of customers and these advantages are more difficult to quantify'.[2] It is precisely by emphasising the importance customers attached to speed and regularity that subsequent writers have come to challenge these earlier views.

Even when the steam railway appeared, it would be wrong to assume that horse-drawn transport for either passengers or goods was driven off the roads. The iron road took time to reach many parts of the country and during that time it generated much new traffic, not least in the growing towns. There were many more horses – perhaps three times as many – harnessed to vehicles on Britain's roads in the heyday of railways in 1900 than there had been when the first inter-city line opened in 1830 (Thompson). After 1900, when road transport itself came to be mechanised and the faithful but costly horse at last departed from most of Britain's roads, historians have tended to study the new motor transport from the point of view of its effects upon the old railway (Dyos & Aldcroft; Bagwell). There has been little consideration of mechanised road transport's spectacular growth since 1950. Nobody in the last decade of the twentieth century can doubt its great significance. Our intention is to show that it has been of greater importance than is usually realised ever since 1700, if not considerably earlier.

New research on roads and road traffic before the railways

Revision of the earlier, disparaging view of road transport started with Albert's research on turnpike trusts, published in 1972, quickly followed by that of Pawson in 1977. Albert showed that, contrary to the Webbs' conclusions, turnpikes formed a connected system of improved roads over long distances, particularly on routes to and from London, much earlier than had been supposed. By 1750 the turnpiking of the seven main roads out of London, which opened out into thirteen major trunk routes, had been largely completed to places as far away as Berwick, Manchester, Chester, Shrewsbury, Hereford, Bristol, Portsmouth and Harwich (Albert, *31–43*).

Pawson (1977) sought to trace not only the direct effects of turnpikes on road transport, but also their indirect effects upon the economy. Other historians have demonstrated the sheer quantity of freight services and the rate at which their number increased. The two complementary approaches here have been, on the one hand, the counting of public, scheduled services, notably the work of Chartres, Turnbull and Gerhold on urban, and particularly London, directories (Chartres, 1977; Aldcroft & Freeman, Ch. 3; Gerhold, 1988), and, on the other hand, the gathering together of all available evidence, mostly non-quantitative, for the traffic of a particular region, exemplified by Hey's work on Derbyshire and south Yorkshire. The role and importance of road transport have also been studied through the records of businesses which used it (Freeman, 1980; Turnbull, 1982), and in two cases the records of road haulage companies (Turnbull, 1979; Gerhold, 1993a).

In general, this recent research, with the notable exception of Hey's work, has concentrated upon public services following fixed routes on specified days and at regular times by common carrier or stage coach. Specially agreed or occasional consignments of goods and passenger travel by private vehicle or horse are much more difficult to investigate, and await further study. We concentrate here upon goods transport. The importance of coach traffic, though inadequately researched so far, has never been in doubt and does not, therefore, require so much discussion.

The picture that emerges is complicated, as we shall see. Freight charges by road were certainly higher than those by water, although water transport involved additional costs such as wharf dues, and sometimes insurance, which narrowed the gap. For example, Jackman found that 'the cost of canal carriage normally did not exceed one-half, and in most cases was from one-fourth to one-third, of the cost of land carriage' (Jackman, *449*). However, reasonably direct water transport was often not available, especially for short journeys. Even more important, goods transport by road was usually faster and was considerably more reliable, with regular timetables along main trunk routes, and this often tipped the scales in its favour. The unreliability of coastal shipping is obvious, and canals were often closed for long periods due to frost in winter, water shortage in summer or for repair (Aldcroft & Freeman, *16*).

Road transport was more suitable for some types of goods than for others. For higher-value goods, including many manufactured items, the cost of carriage by road over 100 or 200 miles amounted to only a few per cent of total cost. Such goods might therefore be sent long distances by road. They included textiles, the most important of Britain's industrial goods, throughout the pre-railway period. On the other hand, for bulky, low-value freights, of which coal and grain are the best examples, transport costs could be a high proportion of total cost. For example, the cost of carrying coal overland for ten miles at least doubled the pithead price in the early eighteenth century. Freights like these had to go by water – at that time by coastal ship and/or river – if they were to be sent longer distances. Even so, the beginning and end of their journeys were often overland to and from navigable water, and road transport was thus an integral part even of these journeys. Heavy goods, like all other freight, were also usually carried overland for the very numerous short journeys. The two modes of transport were largely complementary. The earlier period of Britain's industrialisation was able to proceed without any greater facilities for long-distance bulk transport than were provided by river and coastal waters.

So far as improvement in road transport between 1700 and the 1830s is concerned, we shall see that, while better roads were

Table 1 *Operating costs of carriers and coach proprietors*

Breakdown of costs (per cent)

(1) Oxford–London waggons, c. 1700
(2) Oxford–London waggons, 1825
(3) Manchester/Leeds–London coaches, 1760–1
(4) Coaches running into Liverpool, 1829

	(1)	(2)	(3)	(4)
Provender	68	47	62	40
Harness & shoeing	7	5	*	6
Depreciation of horses	3	4	7	4
Horse-keepers	3	3	5	6
Waggoners/coachmen and postillions	6	9	11	#9
Book-keepers and porters	4	7		
Waggons/coaches	8	6	10	#5
Rent	1	4	–	2
Tolls	0	14	5	10
Tax	n/a	n/a	n/a	18
	100	99	100	100

* Harness is included in the figure for coaches.
# No figures provided in the original breakdown and therefore estimated here.
Sources:
(1) Gerhold, 'Packhorses'.
(2) Gerhold, *Road Transport*.
(3) Exchequer depositions, Public Record Office, E133/8 Geo III Easter 10.
(4) Samuel Salt, *Statistics and calculations essentially necessary to persons connected with railways or canals* (1845), p. 83.

highly important, the real key to the changes was the horse, a large and expensive animal to feed and to keep, with a fairly short working life when it formed part of a team pulling a heavy waggon or a fast coach. Table 1, which shows the operating costs of carriage and coach proprietors at various dates, highlights the dominance of horse costs. As we explain below, improved roads and easier gradients reduced the number of horses per ton hauled; and improved horse breeding was capable of providing sturdier horses which ate less and worked harder – the equivalent in present-day terms of better engines and more miles per gallon.

Parts 1 and 2 examine first the various types of road haulage of goods, describing the roles carrying services performed and how these services changed, and then the carriage of passengers by road, taking the story in each case up to the start of the railway age.

Part 1
Goods transport to the 1830s

Common carriers have been studied mainly from lists of their services in national and local directories. These usually indicate days of arrival and departure and therefore the frequency of services. Recent work has divided common carriers into three categories – London, provincial and local – although in terms of length of route and number of horses the first two categories overlapped (Aldcroft & Freeman, *82–3*).

London carriers

The London carriers are much the best recorded not only in directories but also in advertisements, legal proceedings and business records. Two lists of the late seventeenth century record about 345 services a week (excluding services of under 20 miles distance), and, allowing for omissions, the real figure may have been about 400. All English counties other than the most remote ones – Northumberland, Durham, Cumberland and Cornwall – already had direct services to London, and there were services to Flintshire and Monmouthshire.[3] There were long-established transfer points such as Exeter and York for conveyance to remoter parts. Even by 1700 the network was of some antiquity: there were at least 200 London carrying firms when the first reasonably comprehensive list was compiled in 1637,[4] and there had been a substantial network as early as the fifteenth century (Turnbull, 1979; Gerhold, 1993a, *5–6*). At the end of the seventeenth century about half of all London services were performed by packhorse and half by waggon. Waggons typically covered about 20 to 25 miles a day, at a speed of about two miles per hour, whereas packhorses were usually faster, sometimes covering about 30 miles a day (Gerhold, forthcoming (b)).

Many carriers serving London became involved in legal proceedings, and information about their businesses is therefore to be found in the records of the courts of Chancery and Exchequer, now at the Public Record Office. Services were always organised from the provincial end rather than from London. The businesses were usually small, although the carriers themselves were mostly men of substance and generally owned land. Alternate services along a particular route were often provided by separate carriers operating independently of one another. For example there were four carriers between Kendal and London in 1690. Each had about a dozen packhorses and set off from Kendal in rotation once every four weeks, taking 10 days each way (excluding Sundays) for the journey. Like London carriers on other routes, they employed men to do the actual driving, but they tended to shadow their horses themselves so as to keep an eye on the drivers and to meet customers and innkeepers on the way. London carriers normally used the same inns on each journey as calling places, and the usual arrangement was for the price of horse feed to be fixed for long periods regardless of fluctuations in market prices. In London, the innkeeper looked after horses and men but the carrier had his own warehousekeeper, who attended to the paperwork and the dispatch and delivery of goods (Gerhold, forthcoming (b)).

Probate inventories suggest that the long-distance packhorse carriers to London typically kept about 15 horses per service in the late seventeenth century, but no doubt extra horses were hired to meet peaks in demand. Short-distance London packhorse carriers tended to have fewer horses – only four in the case of carriers from Horsham in Sussex and Chiddingstone in Kent. Those using waggons typically had a single waggon and team for each weekly service, but in major centres of trade, especially textile towns, where there was more to be carried, it was common to run more than one waggon at a time rather than to put on an extra service. As many as five waggons and 39 horses to pull them were owned by a Frome carrier with a weekly service to London in 1710 – the largest number so far encountered for that period (Gerhold, forthcoming (b)).

The regularity of London carrying services is indicated by a small number of detailed accounts between carriers and their innkeepers in about 1700, which happen to have survived through being quoted at length in legal proceedings.[5] They make clear that directory entries indicating a weekly service really meant *every week without fail, even in winter*. Sometimes it was a day late, but longer delays apparently occurred only during heavy snow or floods. Even when there was snow, the determination to maintain regular services was demonstrated in the case of an early nineteenth-century carrier by the continued dispatch of waggons with larger teams of up to 16 horses (Gerhold, 1993a, Ch. 4). The horse itself imposed strong pressure for regularity. Since a horse had to be fed even when not working, and this was the main cost, there was no advantage in following the coastal vessels' practice of waiting for full loads. Customers, too, exerted pressure, since they were paying a premium price for regularity of service.

The London carrying trade enjoyed considerable growth in the eighteenth and early nineteenth centuries, although the extent of this growth is disputed. Chartres counted the number of services per week recorded in directories of 1637, 1681 and 1715, and he and Turnbull then followed a similar procedure for various years up to 1840 (Chartres, 1977; Aldcroft & Freeman, Ch. 3). Their estimates have been challenged, however, chiefly on the grounds that they had double-counted services and had over-estimated average loads in the later years (Gerhold, 1988). The higher and lower figures are shown in Table 2.

What is not in dispute is that numbers and capacity increased considerably. Even on the lower estimates, services per week multiplied threefold and ton-miles fivefold between 1690 and 1838. The disagreement is chiefly significant as regards road transport's proportion of carriage to London: on the higher figures that proportion increased; on the lower figures it declined in the nineteenth century in the face of increased competition from canals and coastal shipping, including steamships from 1816 (Gerhold, 1988, 392, 404–7).

Growth was concentrated largely in existing firms, giving rise to some substantial businesses providing frequent services. They sometimes even had their own small network of feeder routes. The number of weekly services per London carrier rose from 1.1 to 2.4

Table 2 *Estimates of the growth of the London carrying trade, 1681–1840*

| | Services per week | | Index of ton-miles (1765=100) per week | | Ton-miles |
	Chartres & Turnbull	Gerhold	Chartres & Turnbull	Gerhold	Gerhold
1681	372	346			
1690		348		31	74,700
1705		453			
1715	611		17		
1738		422			
1765	990	493	100	100	243,500
1796–8	1662	565	169	111	269,800
1808		608		113	274,300
1816–18	3246	823	344	140	340,700
1826		1025		152	369,800
1838–40	6113	1093	571	149	362,200

Figures from Chartres (1977), Aldcroft & Freeman, Ch. 3, and Gerhold (1988). Chartres and Turnbull's index of services per week 1715–1840 has been converted to actual services on the basis of Chartres's figure for 1715. Gerhold's figures exclude services covering less than 20 miles to London.

between 1681 and 1838, and for services of 80 miles or over from 1 to 3.9. At the same time, capacity per service rose as packhorses were abandoned and waggons became larger (Gerhold, 1988). Most of these businesses appear to have dated back at least to the seventeenth century, although continuity is often obscured by changes of ownership (Gerhold, 1993a, *16*). For example, the best-documented London carrier, Thomas Russell & Co. of Exeter, which ran from Cornwall, the southern half of Devon and Dorset, dated back at least to 1676, but underwent numerous changes of name. In 1816–21, for which period many of its letters survive, it had daily broad-wheeled waggons drawn by teams of eight horses between Exeter and London, and less frequent services with smaller waggons and teams between Exeter, Plymouth and Falmouth. In all, it used about 200 horses and up to 30 waggons, employed between 60 and 70 staff and had premises in each town on the route. At all times, day and night, year after year, the company always had about nine waggons and teams at work between London and Exeter, strung out along the road at intervals of about 40 miles in each direction (Gerhold, 1993a). Examples of even larger businesses are Pickfords, which chiefly served Manchester and had 400 horses hauling waggons in 1803 (Turnbull, 1977, *27*), and Deacon & Co., serving Yorkshire and Norwich, which claimed in 1838 to have 700 horses, 400 employees and 100 branch establishments.[6]

Little information has so far been collected from the earlier part of our period about the higher-value goods in which these long-distance carriers specialised, but all the available evidence suggests that textiles predominated. In the West Country, not only were some London carriers themselves clothiers, but most brought back payments for cloth from London (Gerhold, 1993a, *13–15*). London carriers also conveyed other light manufactures such as leather and metal products, certain raw materials, for example the more valuable wools, imported luxuries such as spices, and cash (typically carried for a rate of one-half per cent).

Thomas Russell & Co. in 1816–21 provides the best available overview of a London carrier's trade at that time. Six main functions can be distinguished. First, and most important, it carried West Country manufactures to London, both for the city itself and for distribution to other parts of the country. The main items were woollen cloth and sailcloth. A manufacturer near Crewkerne, for example, sent about 20 tons of sailcloth a year to London, mostly for forwarding by sea to south and east coast ports, a good example of the complementary nature of road and water carriage. He usually described his consignments as 'particularly wanted', and warned Russell & Co. on one occasion that delay of some sailcloth to be forwarded to Yarmouth would be 'attended with serious consequences to the persons to whom it was destined as well as myself, as it will occassion [sic] vessels being detained from going to sea'.

'Down' traffic of industrial raw materials to the West Country was less important to the carrier but sometimes crucial for the continued employment of skilled labour in industries remote from both their raw materials and their main markets: skins for gloving, silk for throwing, some wool, and hops, the latter chiefly in September and October when new supplies of hops became available and brewers were anxious to restart brewing after the break during the hottest months. One agricultural raw material – seeds – was carried too, especially in March and April.

Thirdly, Russell's waggons carried West Country agricultural produce up to London, chiefly lightly salted butter, but also some pork, skins, and – a curious sideline – half a ton a week of hair to an 'ornamental hair-manufacturer'. When the London price for lightly salted butter fell, farmers stopped sending it by waggon and instead salted it more heavily, waited for London prices to rise and then sent it by sea – another example of complementarity.

The fourth type of traffic, shop goods (chiefly groceries and drapery), was brought down from the London warehouses. Faster and more reliable transport meant that shopkeepers could keep smaller stocks and fulfil orders quickly, thus saving working capital and reducing the risk of impatient customers cancelling orders. A Dorchester grocer, for instance, wrote in 1816 about his supplies of tea that 'if we can depend on their coming on immediately, we shall rarely have occasion to send for them by coach, but the *very trifling* difference in the expense will otherwise be more than counterbalanced by loss of time & inconvenience'. Supplies to larger shops could sometimes be measured in tons: $4\frac{1}{2}$ tons as a single consignment to a Plymouth draper for example. The waggons also carried goods for gentlemen, such as furniture, carriages and provisions; and, their sixth and final function, conveyed to London the gold and silver bullion brought to Falmouth by the Post Office packet boats.

Thomas Russell & Co. was not necessarily typical. It served a region with declining industries, no canal link to London and only relatively poor coastal services. The firm was untypical in carrying bullion, and probably also in the approximate balance of its 'up' and 'down' carriage (which meant that neither direction was regarded as back carriage). In general, however, the functions it performed probably were typical of London carriers elsewhere, even if the relative importance of the different functions varied. The carriage of agricultural produce, for example, may have been more important for short-distance London carriers. Of course, not everything carried by waggon can be assigned to large and tidy categories: goods in Russell's waggons between 1816 and 1821 included such miscellaneous items as springs for a Honiton coachmaker, bundles of trees, hunting dogs, caged birds, numerous pianos, gunpowder, feathers needed by wigmakers and upholsterers, a crate of marble urgently needed by a stonecutter, a panorama of the Battle of Waterloo, and a corpse.

Carriers operating along the major thoroughfares radiating from London were of great economic importance nationally, but they employed only a small proportion of the total number of horses and waggons used in road haulage throughout the country. Assuming we can trust Thompson's estimate of 151,000 horses in road haulage in 1811 and Gerhold's estimate of the ton-miles of carriage provided weekly by the London carriers in 1808, and assuming, too, that the number of horses kept by Thomas Russell & Co. per ton-mile of capacity was typical of London carriers (Thompson; Gerhold, 1988, *403*; Gerhold, 1993a, *53–5*), the London carriers had fewer than five per cent of the horses then used in road haulage. Their loads were, however, undoubtedly worth more per ton than those of smaller carriers, and they also generated much feeder traffic. Possibly the London carriers' proportion was higher a century earlier before the more rapid growth of provincial towns. Turnbull's study of provincial directories shows that London carriers were providing about a tenth of all scheduled services at major provincial towns during the later eighteenth century, though a higher proportion of service-miles (about half at Manchester in 1772 and a third at Birmingham in 1767) (Turnbull, 1977).

Provincial carriers

Directories for provincial towns do not become available in any quantity until the 1750s. Turnbull has used them to show that there was an integrated system of London and provincial carrying services by the mid-eighteenth century covering most of the country. For example, Birmingham in 1767 had 160 services a week (including its London services), provided by 54 firms. These linked it to places as far away as King's Lynn, York, Newcastle, Lancaster, Manchester, Shrewsbury, Bristol and Southampton, at some of which there were forwarding arrangements to more distant parts. Norwich already had 59 services a week in 1728, Nottingham 22.5 in 1751, Liverpool 30.5 in 1753 and Bristol no fewer than 148 in 1755. These variations may result partly from the differing quality of local directories, but they also seem to reflect realistically the economic importance of each town, the availability of water transport, and the extent and prosperity of its hinterland. One important type of route connected industrial town and port, such as Manchester and Hull, from where there were good coasting services to London. Occasionally we obtain glimpses of capacity as well as frequency. The weekly traffic in and out of Kendal in about 1750 consisted of 298 packhorses, four waggons (reckoned equivalent to 15 packhorse loads each) and three or four 'carriages' (equivalent to 40 packhorse loads),[7] indicating an annual capacity of about 2000 tons. Some of the larger provincial firms operated over several different routes, and directories indicate that there were sometimes interlocking partnerships with other provincial firms or London firms.

In Scotland, where information becomes available only from the later eighteenth century, the most important focus of carriers' routes was Glasgow, Scotland's main commercial centre. Smaller networks centred on Edinburgh, Paisley, Dundee, Perth, Aberdeen and Kilmarnock (Morris). There were also important links between Scotland and England. During the second half of the eighteenth century, for instance, the Leeds linen merchant, John Wilson & Son, depended on deliveries of raw linen from Fife, Angus and Perth. These were sometimes by water, sometimes by road transport and sometimes by a combination of both; the balance between road and water changed from year to year. Turnbull, who has studied Wilsons' records, concluded that the choice of mode depended on 'the ability actually to do the job; the regularity and reliability of the service; and price. Of these price undoubtedly ranked high, but not so high as to swamp the rest: to a business like Wilsons, the value of its transport services lay as much in their quality as in their cost' (Turnbull, 1982, *60*).

There is no reason to regard the provincial services as more recent in origin than the London ones. The earliest of all known common carriers was providing services from Oxford to Winchester and Newcastle, as well as London, in the 1390s (Turnbull, 1979, *3*), and we have already mentioned the considerable traffic from Southampton in the 1440s. Not much evidence has yet been produced of the rate of growth of these provincial services, even in the later years when local directories are available.

Local carriers

Short-distance services of up to 30 miles usually accounted for half to three-quarters of the total number of carrier services to major provincial towns in the eighteenth century (Turnbull, 1977, 25–6). Many local services were of very low capacity, such as that of a Salisbury to Dorchester carrier in 1816 who 'cannot take above 35 cwt as he has but three little horses', and one at Penryn in Cornwall at the same date who had three or four horses 'but they scarcely can bear their own weight' (Gerhold, 1993a, 82, *178*). Capacity, however, reflected the loading available, which could sometimes be greater, particularly where carriers catered for local manufacture. At the beginning of our period, for example, Devon's serge industry gave rise to the carriage of wool from Gloucestershire and the north Devon ports, yarn from the spinning to the weaving areas, and cloth from weavers to fulling mills and local markets, especially Exeter. An Exeter inn during a single week in 1729 accommodated carriers from Moretonhampstead (with 10 packhorses), Yeovil (7 packhorses), Ashburton (17 packhorses), Totnes (13 packhorses) and Okehampton (9 packhorses) (Gerhold, 1993a, 9). Similarly, in the Yorkshire woollen district, carding and combing, spinning and weaving often took place in different places (Freeman, 1982), and so did the different processes in the Midlands iron industry, as we shall see.

   Local carriers charged more per ton-mile than those travelling to and from London. In West Country examples of the late eighteenth and early nineteenth centuries local charges per ton-mile were from 29 per cent to 135 per cent higher (Gerhold, 1993a, *160–1*). The poorer side roads used by local carriers and the proportionately longer time taken in unremunerative loading and unloading may have contributed to this, but the main reason was probably the smaller quantity of goods usually available. Local carriers' services may also have been less regular than London and provincial ones.

One type of local carrier revealed by nineteenth-century directories was the market, or village, carrier, whose purpose, according to Everitt, was 'to unite a market town with the villages of its hinterland, with the local area dependent upon it, and not town with town' (Everitt, 1976, *179*). These were very small businesses indeed, typically using a single horse and a comparatively light vehicle such as a van or cart. They served the local town, rarely more than 15 or 20 miles away, and only on market day. Very often their owners were part-timers, combining carrying with shopkeeping, farming, coal-dealing or some other occupation, and they were always based in the village rather than the town. Village carriers were most common around county towns and agricultural centres, rather than around purely industrial towns, new towns or seaside resorts. They have been studied chiefly for the second half of the nineteenth century, but earlier evidence of them exists. Leicester in 1815, for example, had no fewer than 152 services a week, provided by 116 separate carriers (Everitt, 1976).

Everitt lists four functions performed by these village carriers. They did the town shopping for the village people, in one Leicestershire case obtaining everything from 'sheep-netting to wallpaper, from lamp-oil to cups and saucers, from knitting wool to patent medicines, joints of meat, and pounds of tea', thus extending the market's geographical range. They carried other goods, often to the village shop. They acted as 'a kind of primitive country bus'. And they conveyed country produce to town, chiefly (in Leicestershire at least) poultry, game, rabbits, eggs and dairy produce (Everitt, 1976, *181–3*). Everitt believed village carriers to have multiplied from the later eighteenth century and to have been linked with the beginnings of the village shop. However, it is possible that the earlier directories omitted large numbers of local services (Greening, *162–3*), considering them perhaps beneath their notice or too numerous to bother with. The local carrier certainly has a longer history. Chartres and Turnbull, for instance, have analysed the day book of a local carrier at Maidenhead between 1660 and 1685, who served numerous places up to about five miles from the town in most directions (Chartres and Turnbull, 1975, *35–6*). Villages needed carrying facilities to their market town before the appearance of village shops. How such facilities were provided deserves more investigation.

Private carriers

We have so far been considering common carriers who offered scheduled services for public hire, available to anyone who wished to use them. Much carrying, however, including perhaps *most* local carrying, was organised privately, either on an *ad hoc* basis or more regularly for particular heavy traffics. The private carrier had more flexibility than the provider of scheduled services, but he was nevertheless subject to many of the same restraints. He needed to be able to keep his horses fully occupied, which meant that private carriage was very often provided as a sideline by farmers. He also needed to obtain back carriage if his service was not to be unduly expensive. On the other hand, he might use horses kept chiefly for other purposes and could, therefore, sometimes charge less than the true cost. He was certainly regarded as a restraint on the charges of common carriers (Pawson, *57*; Gerhold, 1993a, *181–2*; Albert, *171*).

Private carriage as a proportion of the whole was more important over shorter distances than long, and tended to decline over time. Long-distance private carrying, for example from Dudley to London, appears to have been common in the early eighteenth century (Albert, *171*), but had largely disappeared a century later. Probably the main reason for this was the increased efficiency and frequency of the long-distance common carriers, who enjoyed economies of scale not available to those who operated only occasionally. Long-distance private carrying might, however, still occur where particular loads were substantial and regular or had special requirements (for example fish to London), and where exceptional loads (such as hops from Weyhill Fair) were likely to overburden the common carriers; above all where back carriage was available (Gerhold, 1993a, *181–2*). *Short*-distance private carrying continued to flourish, in both town and country, and transport equipment was very widely available. In Buckinghamshire in 1798, for example, there was a waggon to every seven and a half households, a cart to every four, and a horse to every 1.7 (Chartres in Mingay, VI, *441*).

There were several distinctive types of private carrying. One was the carriage of stone and minerals – heavy materials for which the transport element in total cost was high – from the place of extraction either to the place of use or to the nearest navigable water. Examples in Derbyshire and south Yorkshire included coal, lead, millstones, building stones, lime and salt (Hey, Chs 5 and 6). Where the quantity to be carried was considerable, special arrangements were made with local farmers, and carrying was often a by-occupation at times when the horses were not needed on the farm. Around some eighteenth-century ironworks, for instance, were farms which existed chiefly to accommodate transport horses and which provided carriage instead of paying rent (R. A. Lewis). The most impressive operation of this kind involved the movement of lead (almost 10,000 tons a year in the 1760s) by packhorse over the hilly 40 miles from Alston in Cumberland to Newcastle, the horses returning with provisions for the workforce (Williams, 25).

Private carriers were also needed for many of the links in the chain of movements within industries between obtaining the raw materials and marketing the finished product. In the iron industry in Derbyshire and south Yorkshire, for example, iron ore and charcoal were conveyed by private carriers to the blast furnaces; pig iron was then transferred several miles to forges, rod and bar iron from the forges to outworkers and slitting mills, bunches of rod from slitting mills to warehouses and thence by means of chapmen to nearby nailers; and finally the bags of nails were distributed (Hey, *127–34*). There were similar successions of transport movements in the textile industries (Freeman, 1982).

There was also 'own carriage' of various sorts: farmers taking produce to market, tradesmen such as butchers making local deliveries, and chapmen and merchants carrying goods for sale. Farmers became better equipped for carriage as an increasing proportion of them acquired waggons in the second half of the seventeenth century and the first half of the eighteenth (Porter). There were over 2500 hawkers and pedlars licensed in England and Wales in 1696–7, and undoubtedly many others unlicensed (Spufford, *14–16*). Most of them had a local circuit, but they also travelled widely to markets and fairs. About five-sixths of them at that date travelled on foot rather than by horse. They played an immensely important role in distributing the new consumer items. We hear, for example, of a Penrith chapman in 1683, from whom 'the local purchaser could buy hollands and cambric from the Low Countries, Bengals, calicoes, and muslins from India, silks, linens which were probably dyed in England, Scotch cloth as a cheap alternative to calico for the new-fangled window curtains, and gloves, muffs, bone-lace, ribbons, combs and band-strings for adornment' (Spufford, *16, 21, 74*). The more substantial traders did not travel on foot but had strings of horses: Defoe wrote of 'a set of travelling merchants in Leeds, who go all over England with droves of pack horses, and to all the fairs and market towns over the whole island . . . 'tis ordinary for one of these men to carry a thousand pounds value of cloth with them at a time'.[8] As the eighteenth century wore on, however, greater use was made of common carriers, as happened, for instance, at Manchester between 1730 and 1770:

When the Manchester trade began to extend, the chapmen used to keep gangs of pack-horses, and accompany them to the principal towns with goods in packs, which they opened and sold to shop-keepers . . . On the improvement of turnpike roads waggons were set up, and the pack-horse discontinued; and the chapmen only rode out for orders, carrying with them patterns in their bags.[9]

Goods transport in towns

The period from 1700 to 1840 saw unprecedented urban development. London grew from about half a million people to 1.9 million. The new provincial centres grew at an even faster rate: Manchester, Liverpool, Birmingham and Glasgow, with populations of only about 10,000 in 1700, had by 1841 reached 235,000; 286,000; 183,000; and 225,000 respectively. In addition to the vast quantities of goods of all sorts entering and leaving these places, a great deal more was moved about within them. Both human and animal power were used. Street porters in London, for instance, carried loads of up to three hundredweight for perhaps three miles, and coster girls bore baskets of apples weighing nearly two hundredweight on their heads for up to 10 miles. There was a slow progression from carrying, to barrows, to use of horses or donkeys.

By the nineteenth century wheeled vehicles were being used increasingly (Freeman & Aldcroft, *135–6*). A growing amount of traffic went from wholesalers to shops, from where these goods had to be carried away again. Barrels of beer were moved in considerable numbers from breweries to public houses as fewer residents brewed their own beer. There was also a vast traffic in coal. In the 1790s more coal went overland from the collieries east of Manchester, for instance, to warm the homes and business premises of that bustling place than was delivered from the Duke of Bridgewater's much-publicised canal, and of course all the coal arriving by canal had to be carried by land from the Duke's wharf at Castlefield to its final destination.[10] In some places, notably London and Bristol, porters, carters and hauliers and their charges were closely regulated from the seventeenth century (Pawson, *41*), a fact which indicates the importance of the services they provided.

The essence of eighteenth-century road transport

Having surveyed the main aspects of public and private carrying, we can now summarise *why* goods were conveyed by road. The first category – heavy goods of low value – went by road either because water transport was simply not available, or because, for many short journeys, road transport saved money by being more direct and eliminating the need for transshipment. Even though transporting coal overland ten miles at least doubled the pithead price, the land-sale of coal exceeded the water-sale at the beginning of our period because the coalfields were widely distributed and thus coal required only short journeys to reach its users.[11] The distance over which it was worthwhile transporting heavy goods (other than as back carriage) depended upon how much they were needed and what alternative supplies were available. The long-distance transporting of lead, for example, would presumably not have occurred if there had been a suitable deposit of lead close to the coast or navigable water. The more usual fate of heavy materials remote from water transport was to be used only locally or not at all. Canals and (to a lesser extent) railways were often intended to release these land-locked resources.

The essence of the other sort of traffic – light goods of high value – was that the consignor *chose* to use road transport, because its greater speed and reliability were worth the higher transport cost. Whereas there were many bulky low-value items which virtually *never* travelled long distances by road (most inorganic raw materials, grain, beer and others), there was no corresponding category of traffic whose long-distance journeys were *always* by road (with a very few high-value exceptions such as bullion and silk). The extra price was only worth paying if the advantages of road transport were needed for a particular consignment. In fact three influences were at work. The first was the nature of the journey, especially whether satisfactory water transport was available (which might vary according to the season). The second was the relationship between the weight and value of the goods. The more valuable the goods in relation to weight, the more the extra cost of road transport was offset by the savings that reliable transport made possible through keeping smaller stocks, the greater the saving in insurance costs compared to sea transport, and the less difference the extra cost made to the total cost of the item. The charge for goods carried by Russell's waggons, for instance, was in most cases only one-half to three per cent of their total cost.

The third influence cut across any tidy correlation between high-value traffic and road carriage: the urgency with which any particular consignment was required. If there was no hurry, there was little point in paying the extra road transport cost, whereas even heavy articles might be sent by road when urgently needed. The major items among Russell's loading, for example, were often only a small proportion of the total quantity sent to or from the West Country, as in the cases of sailcloth, butter and hops, the greater part of which appear to have travelled by sea. Reasons for urgency included the need to fulfil orders quickly before they were countermanded or deadlines were missed; to catch favourable markets and minimise speculative risk; to bring forward the date of payments which were made only upon delivery; to maintain continuous production through a regular supply of raw materials; and to prevent deterioration of perishable goods. By satisfying these needs road transport had a considerably greater importance than the weights conveyed suggest. And, where quicker conveyance made it possible to sell items at a higher price (notably in the case of perishables), what mattered was not the relationship of weight and value but the relationship between the extra price and the extra cost of road transport compared with water transport. The few items in Russell's waggons whose cost of conveyance exceeded about three per cent of value fell into this category.

Change in the carrying trade

Implicit in what has been written so far is the idea of change and improvement in goods transport by road. Road transport was not an industry in which nothing changed from decade to decade, but nor was it an industry in which change was sudden or dramatic. Instead, as Freeman has put it, there was 'one long catalogue of minor improvements and adjustments' (Aldcroft & Freeman, 3).

Better roads were not the only improvement, but they were certainly important. Before the turnpikes, road repairs were provided for under Acts of 1555 and 1563, which required parishioners to work for six days a year on the roads of their parish. From 1618, a series of proclamations and Acts sought to preserve the roads by controlling the use made of them, chiefly by limiting the size of teams drawing wheeled vehicles. The ineffectiveness of the statute labour system has generally been assumed rather than demonstrated, but it was likely to be least effective for major roads across clay soils in country parishes, as on the busy stretch of the Great North Road near Ware for which the first Turnpike Act was passed in 1663. Recent research has made clear that a major reason for turnpiking was the increase in traffic which was causing the busier roads to deteriorate (Aldcroft & Freeman, Ch. 2). The essence of the turnpike system was the transfer of the cost of road upkeep from the parish to the road user through the collection of tolls. Income from tolls could be used both for repairs and for improvements.

The second Turnpike Act was not passed until 1695, but thereafter there was a steady stream of them: by 1730, 57 per cent of the length of the thirteen main roads out of London had already been turnpiked, and by 1750, 88 per cent. From the 1720s several town-centred trusts (controlling all the main roads from a particular town) were also being created, notably at the small ports on the rivers Severn and Wye where traffic was transferred between vessel and vehicle or packhorse – a further reminder of the complementary nature of road and water transport. Trusts spread to the growing textile and coal mining areas of northern England in the 1740s. The major increase in turnpiking, however, occurred between 1750 and 1772, where nearly three quarters of trust mileage was established, including many roads in Wales and Scotland. Subsequent years saw some filling-in of the network, particularly in northern industrial areas between 1789 and 1810. By the mid-1830s, about 22,000 miles, roughly a fifth of all the roads in the country, had been turnpiked or entrusted to Improvement Commissioners. There were then 1116 trusts (Albert, Ch. 3; Pawson, Chs 5 and 6; Chartres, 1989, 5).

Recent historians of the turnpike trusts have sought to establish how effective they were, chiefly by using the trusts' own records and to some extent by identifying their impact on transport services. There appears to have been little improvement in techniques of repair until the nineteenth century, but there was more effective use of existing methods, sometimes with the assistance of professional surveyors. The trusts were not, in general, badly administered, although some mismanagement did inevitably occur. Most trusts paid considerable attention to surfacing, drainage, widening and other aspects even before McAdam and Telford. However the new methods (especially McAdam's of using small angular stones which were bound together by traffic passing over them), the building of new stretches of road (particularly to ease gradients), and the fact that expenditure peaked in the 1820s, all suggest that the main benefits of turnpiking were obtained in the earlier nineteenth century (Albert, Chs 4 and 7; Pawson, Chs 7 to 9; Gerhold, 1993a, *139–41, 197–8*).

How did these improvements benefit road users? They did so chiefly by easing the labour of horses drawing vehicles, both directly, by providing harder, smoother and dryer surfaces and less steep inclines, and indirectly, because of less jolting, which made possible lighter vehicles. Thus fewer horses were needed, or the same number of horses could be used at greater speed. The loads which could be drawn per waggon horse increased by about two and a half times between the seventeenth century and the 1830s (Gerhold, 1993a, *27, 198*), though this reflected stronger waggon horses as well as better roads. The savings were partly offset by tolls, but, as Table 1 shows, these were a minor cost compared with the cost of the horses.

As for the parish roads, parish highway rates became more common, and statute labour was generally commuted by 1750. Figures compiled recently by Ginarlis and Pollard (1988, *205–8*) show a surprisingly high level of such local highway expenditure. According to them, it was not exceeded by expenditure on turnpikes until the 1810s. Hence their cautious conclusion that 'there may well have been some exaggeration of parish incompetence'.

Changes in the means of carriage – from packhorse to waggon and from narrow-wheeled to broad-wheeled waggon – were only partly connected with road improvement. It has often been assumed that packhorses were the dominant form of carriage until the eighteenth century (Pawson, *31, 281–5*), but this is not supported by the evidence. As early as the fourteenth century, two-wheeled carts were dominant, although packhorses remained the main type of carriage in some upland areas. In the late sixteenth and early seventeenth centuries, long before turnpikes, four-wheeled waggons replaced two-wheeled carts on long-distance carrying services, and in the late seventeenth century almost equal numbers of London services were performed by waggons and packhorses (Gerhold, 1993b; Hey, *91*).

The inferiority of packhorses, at least on poor roads, should not be exaggerated. On seventeenth-century roads the load drawn per waggon horse was typically two and a half to three times as much as that carried by each packhorse, but this is only part of the economic equation: packhorses were smaller and ate less (perhaps costing only 60 per cent as much to feed as waggon horses), they were less impeded by hills, and they were generally faster, which allowed the carrier to charge higher rates. Packhorses are likely to have cost about 30 per cent more to operate per ton carried, and the extra charge was often of a similar order. So the advantages of packhorse and waggon to the carrier could be evenly matched; in fact, in the London carrying trade the two were often competing with each other on the same route (Gerhold, 1993b).

The balance tilted decisively towards wheeled transport after about 1700, at least in London carrying. Sometimes the change was caused by improved roads, but occasionally it occurred too early for this to provide the only explanation. Other possible reasons include stronger waggon horses; greater demand for carriage (making waggons viable where there was previously inadequate loading); and new ways of working waggons at somewhat greater speeds. However, once turnpike roads had made it easier for horses to draw vehicles, packhorses could remain economic only where there were still steep gradients. London packhorse services are last recorded in 1758 – from Bristol, where they had probably survived because of their greater speed. By the end of the eighteenth century packhorses were confined to the most remote and hilly areas, such as Cornwall and Cumberland (Gerhold, 1993b).

By about 1760, the more substantial carrying firms had replaced their smaller narrow-wheeled waggons with larger vehicles having broad wheels nine inches or more wide. They were generally drawn by eight horses and sometimes loaded high with as much as six tons of goods. They were encouraged by means of lower tolls and by legislation allowing waggons with wider wheels to carry heavier loads, in the belief that broad wheels would roll the road surface rather than breaking it up. Larger waggons also meant a reduced expenditure on drivers per ton carried. Their great *disadvantage* was that teams became less efficient the more horses they contained. Consequently, the savings from using broad-wheeled waggons appear to have been marginal (Gerhold, 1993a, 64–5). On routes with less traffic, especially short-distance services, smaller waggons and two-wheeled carts continued to be used. The most important subsequent change in vehicles was, as we have noted, that better roads made it possible to build lighter waggons requiring less horse power. One new type of vehicle was the sprung van, designed for relatively high speeds, first used by Pickfords in 1814 (Turnbull, 1979, 66–8).

There were three other important areas of change: better waggon horses, new ways of operating waggons, and larger carrying firms which benefited from economies of scale. William Marshall pointed out in 1790 that selective breeding in the preceding 30 years had resulted in stronger horses which ate less.[12] Draught horses certainly became larger, and the little evidence available concerning the feeding regimes of the London carriers' horses confirms the reduction in provender, which saved perhaps 15 per cent of its cost between about 1720 and 1820.[13] The horse breeder needs to be remembered as well as the road engineer.

The new way of operating was by the simple expedient of

changing teams and waggoners at intervals and running continuously, instead of resting the teams at night. In this way journey times were considerably reduced at modest extra cost. These 'fly waggons' covered 35 to 40 miles a day, compared with the 20 to 25 miles of the ordinary services. The Manchester–London journey time was cut from nine days to five by this means in the 1770s. The fly waggon can be traced back to 1737,[14] but it only became commonplace in the early nineteenth century (Freeman, 1977).

The main economies of scale came not from larger vehicles but from having a more frequent service over a single route, which made it worthwhile to take in hand activities formerly contracted out. In particular, from the second half of the eighteenth century, major carriers began to buy provender themselves instead of obtaining it through innkeepers. The saving from cutting out such middlemen was substantial, though it involved greater outlay in granary rent and interest on stocks. Smiths' and wheelers' work, horsekeeping and bookkeeping were also taken in hand, and dedicated premises were obtained in the larger towns (Gerhold, 1993a, *34–5*).

How did all these changes affect the service offered to customers between about 1700 and 1840? Fly waggons, where introduced, allowed shorter journey times, but otherwise journey times changed little. Better roads reduced the cost of carriage at all speeds, but they only marginally changed the speed at which horse haulage was cheapest. When roads were improved, therefore, the carrier could offer the same speed at a lower price (using fewer horses) or a greater speed at the same price (using the same number of horses). Generally the former was the better business proposition, and only a few waggon services exceeded the usual two miles or so per hour. Customers wanted greater speed, but few were willing to pay the much higher charges. This is illustrated by the fate of sprung vans, which became widespread in the 1820s. Most vans travelled at about six miles per hour, further reducing the Manchester–London journey, for example, to 36 hours. The higher speed necessitated a larger number of horses, used in shorter stages than those of waggon teams, and vans consequently cost about 60 per cent more to operate than waggons. This made it difficult to keep charges below the coaches' parcel rates. According to one carrier, 'on some roads a van will not pay because there are not goods sufficient to pay the extra price'. Most van services disappeared in the 1830s (Gerhold, 1993a, Ch. 9).

The main effect of the change was lower rates of carriage relative both to the carrier's costs and to the value of the goods carried. Rates of carriage have been investigated partly from the limits specified by justices of the peace under legislation of 1692 and 1748, and partly from the more scattered evidence of carriers' actual charges. A complicating aspect is that carriers had different rates per ton-mile for different types of goods and sometimes for different journeys (especially up and down journeys), although these variations tended to be within fairly narrow limits. Albert (1972, Ch. 8) has shown that justices' rates tended to follow changes in provender costs, as actual charges must have done. He concluded, therefore, that they are reasonably reliable as an indication of actual rates. Turnbull (1985) demonstrated by means of detailed work on Yorkshire that the justices' rates there were an effective ceiling on charges, although actual charges were sometimes *below* the level set. Many counties, however, did not set rates at all or, if they did, failed to adjust them at times of high provender costs. In the nineteenth century the justices' rates lost touch with carriers' charges altogether, eventually being regarded as a restraint on luggage rates by *coach*.[15] Nevertheless, the picture they give of variation only within a narrow range during the eighteenth century, despite rising provender costs, is confirmed for the second half of the century by the evidence of actual charges assembled by Jackman (Jackman, App. 7; Pawson, *296*).

The changes in carriers costs and carriers' charges can be compared. Between the West Country and London from about 1690 to the 1830s, the costs (weighted according to their importance in 1690) approximately doubled, whereas rates of carriage appear to have declined slightly, indicating at least a doubling of productivity. Between Leeds and London the same method indicates a trebling of productivity; in other words, charges in the 1830s were a third (or less) of what they would have been without improvements such as better roads. The exact figures should not be too heavily relied on, but they do indicate a substantial gain in efficiency. Between 1690 and 1837 West Country rates of carriage declined by about two-fifths in relation to industrial prices and just over half in relation to agricultural prices, which is likely to have been particularly significant for the heavier goods carried by road, such as seeds, hops, skins and butter. It mattered much less to the higher-value items such as textiles, for which the transport element of total cost was already small. Improved roads may have been the most important single contributor to carriers' increased efficiency; but better horses and economies of scale were both important too (Gerhold, forthcoming (a)).

Similar calculations cannot even be attempted for local carriage because it was too varied. Local carriage undoubtedly changed less than long-distance carriage. However, such gains in efficiency as it did experience are likely to have been especially significant, since local carriers were often moving bulky goods such as coal, whose transport costs were substantial in relation to their value; hence the early turnpiking in the mining areas of Derbyshire and Durham, for example.

Improvements in water transport tended to have more obvious and immediate results than those in road transport, and water transport became much more widespread as canals extended the existing river navigations. Canals removed much of the heavier traffic from roads where there had not previously been an alternative route by navigable river, as between the West Midlands and London. Canal *services* improved markedly in the early nineteenth century, when fly boats became common. Like fly waggons, they used relays of horses, observed regular timetables and often worked all night. Their speeds were faster than waggon speeds, but total journey times were longer because of locks and, often, a less direct route. Between London and Birmingham in 1832, for instance, with a fairly direct canal route, goods took four days by waggon and 'five days; sometimes a week' by fly boat (Gerhold, 1988, *406–7*; Jackman, *437*).

Coastal services became more efficient too, but the increasing *volume* of coastal trade was probably of greater significance. The tonnage of coastal shipping in England and Wales almost quadrupled between 1765 and 1826, and this must have resulted in greater frequency of service and probably greater regularity, especially on the east coast. Services were increasingly advertised as departing at regular intervals whether fully loaded or not. Steamships dramatically increased the attractiveness of coastal services from 1816 onwards: they were both faster and cheaper than waggons, though they served only a limited number of ports, and often at less frequent intervals. Their impact on long-distance carriers (and coach proprietors) operating on roads parallel to the east and south coasts was considerable (Aldcroft & Freeman, Ch. 4; Gerhold, 1993a, *91–2, 198–203*).

Droving

Droving differed from most other overland traffic in that it did not depend on the horse and it avoided roads themselves as far as possible, especially turnpike roads. The drovers preferred open country or by-ways, where grazing was more readily available, where there was less nuisance from other traffic, where they could avoid tolls, and where the animals' feet were not harmed by hard surfaces. It was almost invariably cheaper to transport animals overland than by water transport. As Adam Smith explained, 'By land they carry themselves to market. By sea, not only the cattle, but their food and their water, too, must be carried at no small expense and inconveniency' (Haldane, *20*).

Enormous numbers of animals were conveyed by drovers. In 1771 it was estimated that the livestock killed each year in London included 98,000 black cattle, 195,000 calves, 711,000 sheep and lambs, and 239,000 pigs and swine. In the early eighteenth century 30,000 cattle a year were already being driven from Scotland to England; a century later this number had risen to 100,000 (Fussell & Goodman, *215*; Haldane, *170, 205*).

Regional specialisation and the huge and increasing demand of London and other urban and industrial areas formed the economic basis of droving. Cattle could be bred and reared relatively cheaply in remote areas where the land had little other use. They were often driven first to an area closer to the place of consumption, where they could recover from the emaciating journey and be fattened. The general flow of cattle ran from the north and west to the south and east, but with many local and regional currents. Scottish cattle were driven to northern England and Norfolk; Welsh cattle to the Midlands, Essex and Kent, creating strong links between unlikely places such as Haverfordwest and

Ashford;[16] south Wales and Welsh border cattle to Buckinghamshire; and south-west England and Severn valley cattle to Somerset
(Fussell & Goodman, *216*).

Scotland and Wales only ever supplied a small proportion of the
cattle consumed in England, and the importance of the London
market should not be exaggerated either. However, the Scottish
cattle droves have been the most thoroughly studied by historians.
In 1801, Galloway cattle

are mostly bred upon the moors or hilly country and grazed upon the
lands nearer the sea, until rising four or five years old, when the graziers
and drovers take them up in great numbers to the fairs in Norfolk and
Suffolk previous to the turnip-feeding season, from whence the greatest
part are again removed in the Winter and Spring (when fat) to supply the
amazing consumption of the capital. (Bonser, *50*)

Many Scottish cattle came from much further north, from the
highlands and islands, often having to swim the first part of the
journey. The beasts were gathered at 'trysts' on the edge of the
highland area. Droves might consist of 100 to 300 beasts or more
(sometimes thousands in the nineteenth century), and one drover
travelling on foot usually took charge of 50 or 60 animals. The
chief drover might take the beasts on his own account (often on
credit), on commission or for a daily wage. It was important not to
hurry the animals, and a usual day's journey was 10 to 12 miles in
the uplands; 15 miles or more in the lowlands. The droves were to
be seen from May to October, but chiefly in the autumn. Droving
depended above all on wayside grazing and undisturbed rest, food
and water at night; the drovers preferred the higher ground where
grazing was more freely available. Highland drove roads had
recognised stopping places called 'stances' (Haldane, Ch. 2).

Detailed accounts of six droves between the East Riding of
Yorkshire and London in 1688–9 reveal a smaller-scale trade, with
an average of only 18 beasts per drove, although how typical this
was is not known. The cattle driven in February covered 15 miles
per day (Woodward). Sheep were also driven in large numbers.
They followed the same general lines as the cattle, but sheep
breeding was more widespread than cattle rearing. The most
important flows by the nineteenth century may have been from
Wales to England. Pigs too were driven from Wales (some having

72896

come first from Ireland) and from Cornwall to London and elsewhere, covering only six to ten miles a day. Up to 2000 geese and turkeys at a time were marched from Norfolk, Suffolk and Cambridgeshire to London, between August and October. In the latter month, according to Defoe, 'the roads begin to be too stiff and deep for their broad feet and short legs to march in' (Fussell & Goodman, *225–36*; Haldane, *199–200*; Bonser, *53–5*).

The main costs of droving appear to have been grazing, drovers' wages and turnpike and bridge tolls. For example, the breakdown of costs for a cattle drove from Hereford to Hitchin in 1838 was 47 per cent for grass, 28 per cent for drovers' wages and keep and 21 per cent for tolls; and for a mid-nineteenth-century sheep drove from Falkirk to Cumberland it was 53 per cent for grass, 30 per cent for drovers' wages and 17 per cent for tolls (Colyer, *66*; Bonser, *87*). High costs were incurred keeping the animals at their destination if they could not immediately be sold (Colyer, *67*). In a number of examples from about 1700 the total costs averaged about $4\frac{1}{2}$ per cent of the animals' final sale value; whether this proportion later changed significantly is not known (Chartres, 1985, *468*). However, droving also resulted in a substantial loss of weight – one third according to an estimate relating to cattle driven from Galloway to Norfolk.[17] There were substantial risks too, particularly of cattle plagues and the collapse of prices at the destination; variations in demand at the intended market seem to have been the main influence on profit (Colyer, *64, 74–5*).

Droving became increasingly difficult during the eighteenth and nineteenth centuries. Enclosure and other developments were reducing the availability of free grazing. In the second half of the eighteenth century it was becoming necessary to pay even for highland stances (Haldane, *207–10*). Tolls became increasingly significant and brought no corresponding benefit; indeed, harder roads made it even more necessary for cattle to be shod. The general growth of road traffic must also have been unhelpful. On the other hand, the demand for meat increased relentlessly and the price of cattle rose. At Smithfield, London, for example, the number of cattle sold per year increased from 75,000 in the 1740s to 165,000 in the 1830s, and sheep from 554,000 to 1,283,000.[18]

Alternatives to droving grew in importance in the first half of the nineteenth century. Carriage of carcases by cart or van is likely to have increased, especially when fast sprung vans became common in the 1820s. Steamships were conveying live cattle from Scotland to London from the 1820s, but it is not clear how significant these alternatives were. When railways appeared, they quickly captured the droving traffic, often carrying carcases rather than live cattle; but they were slow to penetrate the breeding areas. The peak year for Scottish droving was 1835, but St Faith's market near Norwich continued until 1872 (Haldane, *204, 217–20*; Bonser, *126, 225–9*).

The significance of road transport

The significance of road transport has been difficult for historians to assess for two main reasons. The first is that there was no dramatic or sudden change in what it did, or how well it did it, and therefore no obvious *new* contribution to the economy such as can be seen with the spread of canals and railways. For example, a national market in textiles, undoubtedly dependent on road transport, already existed as early as the fifteenth century. The second is that, unlike canals and railways, some form of road or track has always been available virtually everywhere. The best tribute to a ubiquitous form of transport is precisely its lack of influence on the location of economic and other activity, whereas in the case of canals and railways historians have been able to assess their impact by comparing places with and without them.

Moreover, as we have seen, the significance of road transport before the railways cannot be measured by the *volume* of goods carried. The *value* of goods carried would be a better guide, if figures were available; but this too would under-state the significance of road transport, since even where only a small proportion of some commodity went by road, that small proportion was sometimes of disproportionate significance. The mere *possibility* of conveying goods quickly in an emergency enabled tradesmen to keep smaller stocks and manufacturers to retain regular customers in distant places. This emphasises again the complementary nature of road and water transport, not so much in carrying different commodities as in satisfying different needs.

Another way of assessing the significance of road transport is to identify the economic functions or developments for which it was partly or chiefly responsible. These included the conveyance of textiles (the country's most important manufacture throughout the period) to their markets, assisting the marketing of the vast range of products which made up the 'consumer revolution'; the carriage of food to the growing towns; promoting the regional specialisation of agriculture and industry; enabling money to be transferred around the country at reasonable cost; making it possible for London to dominate the national economy; providing the vital short-distance links to and from navigable water; and carrying materials between the sites of the different processes within industries such as textiles and iron. Water transport was well suited to high-capacity flows, for example of inorganic raw materials from mine to city wharf, but was less able to serve widely dispersed industrial and agricultural production or the general needs of commerce (Wrigley). The chronology of transport development must also be borne in mind: as Chartres and Turnbull have observed, 'Britain industrialised without the railway, and for much of the period even canals were of limited value' (Aldcroft & Freeman, *97*); there was no 'canal system' until a direct link with London was provided in 1805.

Earlier historians underestimated the value and significance of road transport; but we must not make the opposite mistake of exaggerating road transport's ability to serve all the needs of the economy. The needs it was failing to serve became more obvious when alternative forms of transport became available. For example, the pottery and iron-making industries of the Midlands, not situated on navigable rivers, grew massively when canals were built (Bagwell, *23*). The railways satisfied a desire for greater speed which neither road nor water transport could provide. Chartres concludes, very fairly, that 'road transport could not have sustained the completion of the steam–coal–iron industrial revolution, but it may have been the critical transport element in the cumulative growth which formed its background' (Chartres, 1989, *8*).

Part 2

Passenger transport to the 1830s

Greater change than in goods transport

Passenger transport, unlike goods, was conducted almost exclusively by road. The main exceptions, both chiefly of the nineteenth century, were (i) passenger boats on some canals, especially where (as in Scotland) they connected populous districts and had few locks, and (ii) steamships, which from the 1820s were a threat to coaches running parallel to the south and east coasts. On these limited routes both canal boats and steamships could provide stage-coach speeds for much less than stage-coach prices (Bagwell, *28–31, 62*).

Passenger transport by road experienced much greater change than goods transport. At the beginning of our period, most passenger travel appears to have been on horseback, and there were still people who regarded it as effeminate for a man to ride in a vehicle. Nevertheless, some passengers travelled in carriers' waggons or by stage-coach. Coaching was still a young industry in 1700. Coaches as such in England date back to the mid-sixteenth century, but the first public scheduled service was recorded in 1637, and long-distance coaches seem to have originated in the late 1650s (Jackman, *109–22*). A list of 1690 records 420 services to and from London every week, and is undoubtedly incomplete. Most of them were short-distance: only 119 a week were to places more than 40 miles from the capital.[19] London-bound services comprised virtually the entire coaching stock, for there were hardly any others in the provinces. Coaches could survive only on the busiest routes.

The economics of coaching were the economics of working

horses at faster than the optimum speed for horse-drawn vehicles, which was between two and three miles per hour. Greater speed necessitated a larger number of horses or smaller loads (or both), and therefore resulted in higher costs. As speeds increased, costs rose more than proportionately. When about eleven miles per hour was reached the horse could do little more than move its own body. At that speed coach horses typically worked only an hour a day, and were quickly worn out. Such high speeds depended on passengers' willingness to pay high fares.

Greater speed was much more expensive on a poor road than a good one. Consequently coaches were not at first much faster than packhorses or even waggons. The London to Exeter coach of c. 1700 seems to have been typical in covering 44 miles a day in summer, although from the beginning of coaching there were also 'flying coaches'. Unlike flying waggons these did not run all night, but covered longer distances per day (such as London to Oxford) by virtue of longer hours and an occasional change of horses. The poorer state of the roads in winter made a big difference. There is plenty of evidence of coaches running winter as well as summer; but flying coaches ceased to fly in winter and other coaches lengthened their journey times – in the Exeter case from four days to six.[20]

The Exeter coach of c. 1700 required fewer horses per mile covered than contemporary Exeter waggons because the horses were drawing a much lighter load: a vehicle containing up to six passengers rather than one loaded with several tons of goods. The small payload meant that coach fares were high: London to Exeter cost 40/- or 45/- in the late seventeenth and early eighteenth centuries, or about 3d a mile, probably three times the charge for a passenger by waggon (Gerhold, forthcoming (b)). This appears to explain why the coach trade grew only slowly for much of the eighteenth century (Aldcroft & Freeman, 69). Speeds were too low and fares too high to attract a much larger clientele: not enough people were willing to pay the even higher fares which would have made possible greater speeds.

Circumstances changed, however, in the final quarter of the eighteenth century. There was a huge increase in the number of coaches, accompanied by drastic reductions in journey times. According to Jackman, journey times by the fastest coaches fell to between a third and a fifth of their former level between 1750 and 1830. The sharpest reductions were between about 1750 and 1780. For example, London to York by the fastest available coach took four days in 1754, three days by 1761 and 36 hours by 1774. Thereafter the acceleration was less impressive: 29 hours by 1818, 24 hours by 1825 and 20 hours by 1836 (Jackman, *335–6, 339*). By the 1770s, seasonal timings were disappearing, although there undoubtedly continued to be higher costs in winter. Services also became more diversified, with a range from the cheaper 'slow coaches' and caravans to the more expensive flying coaches (Pawson, *292, 297–8*).

Flying coaches were soon travelling faster than the men on horseback who carried the post. In 1784, John Palmer made a successful bid to carry the mails by coach between Bristol and London. The experiment was such a success that mail coaches soon began to run on the other main routes. They had their own armed guards and paid no turnpike tolls. At the sound of the guard's post horn, turnpike gates had to be thrown open in readiness and all other vehicles had to give way anywhere along the road. The number of passengers was limited to ensure high speed, but these passengers could be charged high fares for a premium service (Vale). Mail coaches were not notably faster than the others ($7\frac{1}{4}$ miles per hour at first), but they set new standards of reliability, indicated by the example of 'two mails in opposite directions, north and south, starting at the same minute from points six hundred miles apart, [which] met almost constantly at a particular bridge which bisected the total distance' (Vale, *1*). By 1836, mail coach timings on the 16 main routes averaged 9.2 miles per hour (including stops), the fastest being 10.3 miles per hour, a speed then exceeded by a few other coaches (Austen).

Greater speed without massive increases in fares opened up a vastly expanded market for passenger travel. Chartres and Turnbull's figures indicated a fourfold increase in the number of London services between 1773 and 1796, and even faster growth in passenger miles, followed by only modest growth during the early nineteenth century (Aldcroft & Freeman, *69*). On some roads coaches became very numerous and competition was intense. At the same time the capacity of stage coaches increased – from the usual six passengers inside in about 1700 to six insiders and up to twelve outsiders (the maximum allowed by law) in the nineteenth century.

Provincial coach networks also developed rapidly in the last quarter of the eighteenth century. Freeman's study of south Hampshire (1977) traced their growth by means of advertisements, directories and turnpike and other records. There was dramatic expansion there in the late eighteenth century, especially in the 1770s, followed by a period, from 1798 to 1823, when the pattern remained substantially unchanged (perhaps reflecting the dearness of provender), and then by further expansion, chiefly on existing routes, after 1823. By 1839 the range of services had grown five-fold since 1775, and at Southampton about a thousand people were entering and leaving by coach every day. Reductions in journey times tended to occur in phases: on the London–Southampton route, for example, in 1780–90 and 1815–27. Freeman noted that 'whilst there was a generally universal fall in coach journey times over the period as a whole, the precise timing of such reductions was the product of a complex set of prevailing local conditions'. His work emphasises the need for more regional studies. According to Bagwell (43), the number of coach services from ten sample urban centres multiplied eightfold between 1790 and 1836. By the latter date the number of passenger journeys made annually nationwide may have reached no fewer than 10,000,000.

Stage coach expansion explained

What accounts for the huge expansion of stage coaching? Demand is likely to have increased as incomes rose, and, with greater economic activity and a rapidly growing population, more people needed to travel, for business and other reasons. But the main explanation seems to be that coachmasters were able to provide greater speed without a prohibitive increase in fares, despite the imposition of mileage duty in 1779 and its subsequent increases. In 1838 one coachmaster observed significantly that the public were 'more careful, on a large scale, about their time than about their money' (Bagwell, *141–2*). Information on coach fares is sparse: on some routes they appear to have been stable for long periods (except at times of especially intense competition); on others they rose significantly, though usually less steeply than provender prices or the general price level (they almost doubled in south Hampshire between the 1770s and 1820s) (Aldcroft & Freeman, *78*; Dickinson; Freeman, 1977, *278*). Fares certainly rose far less than they would have done if greater speed had been obtained simply by using more horses in shorter stages. The number of horses required rose only from 0.6 per double mile (i.e. a coach each way daily) in the case of the Exeter coach running at four or five miles per hour in 1690 to about 1.0 or fewer per double mile for a coach running at ten miles per hour (and carrying many more passengers) in the 1830s.[21] Better, specially-bred horses and improved vehicles are likely to have contributed to this; in particular, Elliot's elliptical spring of 1804 permitted a lower centre of gravity. This made possible safe travel at higher speeds for more outside passengers (Bagwell, *48–9*). Longer running hours per day and – certainly not to be forgotten – the increasing incidence of night running were as important, or almost as important, as greater speed in reducing journey times. As Jackman observed, whereas the rate of travelling at least doubled between 1750 and 1830, journey times fell to a third or a fifth of those in 1750 (Jackman, *339*).

There is, nevertheless, little doubt that the increased speeds and great expansion of coaching depended chiefly on better roads, which were much more important for passenger transport (on account of the higher speeds) than for the long-distance carriage of goods. Both improved surfaces and reduced gradients were vital for reducing the exertion of coach horses and, therefore, for restraining the rise in costs as speed increased. Not surprisingly, the great era of improvement and growth in the coach trade closely followed the peak period for setting up turnpike trusts (c. 1750–72). The turnpikes also made possible some of the other changes in the coach trade. Night running may well have been too dangerous at speed on very poor roads, and passengers might have been more reluctant to endure up to 24 hours a day of jolting over rough, ill-made roads. (It was uncomfortable enough even after road improvements.) Moreover, as with good waggons, improved roads made possible lighter vehicles, which therefore required less horse power. They also made it possible to use a different type of horse. Instead of needing four or six heavy horses to drag a coach through the mud, coachmasters could now use teams of four horses better suited to galloping at speed for distances of ten miles or so (Gerhold, forthcoming (a)).

The beneficial effects of improving the roads could not have increased indefinitely, however. Further reductions in costs were possible; but the turnpikes' effects on speed were exhausted on some routes in the 1820s and on others in the 1830s because the maximum speed at which horses were capable of drawing vehicles, even for short periods, had been reached (Freeman, 1975, *278–9*; Gerhold, 1993a, *188*).

Coaches were operated by partnerships of innkeepers who had been involved in coaching from its beginnings and by the late eighteenth century utterly dominated it. It was a much less demanding business than goods carrying and was therefore more easily pursued as a sideline, and a sideline more directly relevant to the innkeepers' business of providing food and accommodation. After payment of joint costs, which included tolls, coachmen's and porters' wages, the taxes imposed on coaches, and 'mileage' (the payment for hiring the vehicles), receipts were divided between the partners along each stage of the route in proportion to the work done by their horses. With his share each individual partner had to cover his costs in horsing the coaches through his particular stage. Profit depended chiefly on his success in buying provender at the best prices and finding suitable horses, and on the partnership's success in booking passengers (Bovill, *130–8*). Profits were sometimes high; but it was a business of considerable risk because of the often intense competition, which sometimes temporarily reduced fares below cost. A large organisation was, however, less vulnerable to fierce competition than a small one, and services were increasingly concentrated in the hands of a few major innkeepers, especially at the London end. In the 1830s, Chaplin of London had 1800 horses and 2000 employees, and horsed 60 coaches, including 14 of the 27 mails out of London. In 1836 the three largest coachmasters in London horsed 275 of the 342 services a week (Bagwell, *50*). More research is needed into various aspects of this large and flourishing industry: the booking arrangements; coach building in London's Long Acre, coach maintenance at Millbank; and their provincial counterparts.

Other forms of passenger transport by road

Stage coaches were not, of course, the only form of passenger transport. At the upper end of the market, the posting system involved the hire of horses, and sometimes post-chaises, from innkeepers or postmasters to carry passengers to the next posting house, where the horses would be changed. Travellers might hire horses and post-chaise, horses to draw their own carriage, or riding horses. Travelling post, even with one's own carriage, was at least twice as expensive as travelling by stage coach. Yet on some roads in the 1830s as many people travelled post or by hired gig as by stage coach (Bagwell, *54*). Post-chaises were also used to link places off the main roads with coach services. Two-wheeled gigs were much favoured by riders out, the commercial travellers of their day, who often visited customers over a wide area, sending orders back to their employers by mail.

Some forms of passenger transport declined in importance. Carriers had once had an important role in passenger transport, both hiring out hackney horses and conveying passengers in their waggons. Some of the earliest fly waggons were intended chiefly for passengers, and at 40 or so miles a day were not much slower than coaches had been in the mid-eighteenth century. However, as coaches became faster, the waggons were left with only the poorest passengers. Riding on horseback also declined. By the 1820s it was no faster than travelling by stage coach (Bagwell, *49*).

For local transport, poorer people continued to walk or use the village carrier. The better-off increasingly used private carriages instead of riding on horseback. As for the towns, most, even the largest, were still small enough, even in the 1830s, for walking to remain the main form of travel. London, of course, had the most developed passenger transport system. The number of hackney coaches permitted there rose from 700 in 1694 to 1200 in 1832. A substantial network of short-stage coaches also developed, serving suburban villages and neighbouring towns. It grew considerably from the mid-eighteenth century and by 1825 was providing about 1800 journeys a day to and from the City and West End. There were, too, innumerable private carriages: 4255 four-wheelers and 2909 two-wheelers in 1754, whereas even a substantial provincial city like York then had only 116 and 214 respectively (Jackman,

127–30). Sedan chairs existed not only in London but in some provincial cities, and had advantages in providing a personal and flexible service over short distances, especially in narrow, crowded streets. Their disappearance in the early nineteenth century has been attributed to street widening.

Contribution to economic growth

It would be easy to regard passenger travel as having less economic significance than goods transport, but this was not necessarily the case. It is true that coach travel was often undertaken for pleasure. As the flourishing coach trade on the Bath road most clearly demonstrates, coaches were an important aspect of the 'consumer revolution' of the eighteenth century, bracketed by Chartres with the spa, the teacup and the printed cotton (Chartres, 1989, *8*). Even in this respect they had considerable economic significance, as the growth of resorts, spas and county towns emphasises. Stage coaches also had three very important business functions, crucial to the process of economic growth. First, they carried small parcels such as samples, patterns and bundles of banknotes. Secondly, as we have seen, from 1784 they carried the post, including market information, orders, invoices and newspapers. Thirdly, and perhaps of greatest significance, they moved businessmen around the country, as they sought to widen their market or take personal control of deals formerly made at a distance through agents. The number of passengers carried by coach might be small in relation to total population (for example about 7000 a week out of 315,000 in south Hampshire in the 1830s (Freeman, 1975, *276*)), but it was the most economically active who travelled. These aspects of coach travel and their impact on business organisation and efficiency need more study. They were clearly important in the development of a modern industrial state. The stage coaches were significant too in originating the idea of regular, frequent passenger transport between towns and providing a ready-made passenger market for the railways (Aldcroft & Freeman, *64*).

Part 3
Road transport in the railway age

Horse-drawn road transport, despite its higher cost per ton-mile, continues to grow

We have stressed that it was the cost of keeping horses which made road transport so expensive. From the beginning of the seventeenth century, attempts had been made, with some success but with limited geographical application, to reduce these costs by building special railroads, the smooth surfaces and lower rolling resistance of which allowed horses to pull heavier loads than they could along ordinary roads. These railroads (or railways) usually carried coal from pithead to navigable water. The investment of fixed capital saved working capital. In the early nineteenth century, when the horse – costly in working capital – began to give place to the steam locomotive on these colliery lines and a sturdier infrastructure was involved, more fixed capital was needed. This enabled even heavier loads to be moved at lower cost and – the unexpected surprise when an improved locomotive was produced at the Rainhill Trials in 1829, on the eve of the opening of the world's first intercity railway, from Liverpool to Manchester – at higher speed.

Intercity railways could not have been contemplated without the considerable road traffics already generated along the main trunk routes by the waggons and coaches. The large capital sums raised by the new railway companies depended on these existing vast traffic flows to make their economies in operation remunerative, and much was made of these traffic figures in all railway prospectuses. The railways also learned much from the earlier experience and organisation of road haulage men and coach operators. Indeed, some railways enlisted their help, as we shall see.

Because of the locomotive's unexpected speed, the steam railway was able to win the passengers and higher-value goods traffic which had been carried by road as well as the bulky, lower-value freight which had depended on water transport. In fact, the latter, and especially the steam-powered coastal vessels, were better able to withstand the new competition. The railways' share of the important coal trade from the north-east to London, for instance, was little more than half of that growing traffic as late as 1870. And even without steam power, canals could not only maintain, but increase, their business for some time by cutting their rates. During the earlier 1840s, for instance, the waterways between Liverpool and Manchester were carrying more than twice the tonnage of the new railway (Hadfield & Biddle, *125*). On the other hand, railways had an overwhelming cost advantage, as well as a speed advantage, when competing *directly* on stage coach or hauliers' routes for passengers and higher-value freight which went by road. Fourteen of the 26 coaches running between Liverpool and Manchester had been withdrawn by the end of 1830, three months after the railway's opening, even though the company ran only four trains a day, and was suffering considerable teething troubles. By 1832, only one coach was left and that carried mainly parcels (Carlson, *239, 243*; Simmons, *31*).

It should not be deduced from this, however, that all horse-drawn road transport was instantly doomed. It took time to build even the main lines. London was not connected to the Liverpool–Manchester railway until 1838 or to Glasgow and Edinburgh until a decade later. While Britain can be said to have had a railway system linking its main traffic centres by the early 1850s, many more lines still remained to be built to other places. To the 6700 route miles open in 1851, another 11,000 were added by the mid-1890s. Much traffic remained for coach proprietors and hauliers until these directly competing lines were opened. The wealthy used their own coaches, which gave greater privacy, hiring horses from post houses en route on longer journeys. More prosperous farmers showed off their new gigs; less prosperous ones travelled in locally-made spring carts (Bagwell, 1981, *32*).

The road transport men quickly adapted to change, redeploying their resources, filling the gaps in the system and working with the railways as they had long been accustomed to work with water transport. Two of the leading London coach firms, Chaplin and Horne, for instance, joined together, threw in their lot with the newcomer and in 1840 became London collection and delivery agents for the Grand Junction Railway. The long-distance carriers took advantage of the new railways and almost immediately transferred their freight to them. They provided book-keeping, porterage and cartage, operated connecting services and bore the risk, while the railways provided track, locomotive power and rolling stock (together four-fifths of the total cost). When the railways became better established, however, and saw advantage in taking over the carriers' remaining role and operating their own road transport services, they had no difficulty in doing so. Most of the independent carrying businesses disappeared in the 1850s. The great exception, Pickfords, which had branches in many parts of the country and had opened a warehouse by the canal at Camden Town, London, to receive goods by water, would have shared the same fate had it not also put its services at the disposal of the London & North Western Railway in 1847, thus saving the company from some of the burden of acquiring horses, stables, vehicles and receiving offices (Turnbull, 1979, Chs 6 and 7).

As their network developed, the railways captured more and more of the longer-distance passenger and freight traffic which would otherwise have gone by road; but in the process they also generated more short-distance road traffic. And, in so far as railways cut transport costs, they encouraged traffic growth in general and the growth of towns in particular. By the end of the century, Britain was the most urbanised of the developed countries with about 80 per cent of its population living in towns. Most of their inhabitants moved about to a large extent on foot, as they still do (Hillman & Whalley, *19*). And, for much of the nineteenth century, wage earners in particular had to walk many miles a day because they could not afford to ride. Twenty-eight miles per day for six days a week has been verified in one case (Glos. Community Council, 1950, *14*). It was the better-off, perhaps one-third of the population, who travelled more and more in horse-drawn vehicles within the towns, along country lanes and to and from railway stations. The latter might involve long journeys until branch lines were built. Many people still living in villages or scattered throughout the countryside were wholly dependent either on their own two feet or on horse-drawn transport if they needed to ride or if heavier goods had to be transported.

Omnibuses and hackney carriages for the middle classes

While the steam railway was being developed in the north-east of England in the 1820s, attempts started to be made to move road vehicles by steam power in London, then the centre of steam engine manufacture. These trials, associated particularly with Goldworthy Gurney and Walter Hancock, were continued there and elsewhere, mainly in southern England, until 1836. They failed partly because of the cost of running upon toll roads but mainly because the roads could not bear the great weight of the relatively inefficient, low-pressure steam engines of the day. They required a more substantial railway track to carry them (Nicholson, I, Chs 2 and 3; Barker & Thompson, *11-13*; James). Even when lighter, more efficient steam engines were developed later in the century and road surfaces were much improved, steam traction on roads was only a limited success.

Improvements in passenger transport by road, especially in and around the growing towns, came in types of vehicle and not in means of traction. Stage coaches had been carrying passengers from the outskirts into London from the seventeenth century; but, with seats inside for only four or six people, they were not suitable vehicles for such short journeys: most passengers had to keep climbing up and down to and from the roof. Fares were high – as much as 18 to 24 old pence per single journey in the 1820s. Specially-adapted vehicles with dickey seats at the back saved much of this climbing: but even these so-called short stages did not meet the need. A rectangular box on wheels, carrying more passengers inside and sheltered from the weather, was much to be preferred.

The omnibus, bearing a French name because it was developed in Paris, was introduced to London's busiest short-stage route in 1829 by George Shillibeer, a Londoner who had business interests in the French capital. It was soon taken up by other London proprietors, especially after 1832 when the regulations were relaxed to allow picking up and setting down in the central streets. It was usually a two-horse vehicle carrying 14 passengers inside with a few hardy gentlemen opting to sit on the edge of the roof at the front by the coachman. Omnibuses, locally manufactured with local variations in design, all privately owned and operated, very soon made their appearance in other British towns. After 1843, with changes in the method of levying mileage duty, it became usual to place two seats lengthwise along the open roof, reached from the back by vertical ladder. In this form two horses could pull a vehicle capable of carrying 25 people, all seated; but the work was heavy, the horses had to be rested regularly and on the busiest routes a stud of 11 horses per bus was needed. Nevertheless, changes in bus design and taxation allowed fares to be reduced from Shillibeer's 12 or 6 old pence per ride to as little as two old pence for the shortest journeys by mid-century. This was still too expensive for the mass of the population, however, for most of them, even when in regular work, earned only about 240 old pence a week or less. Vast numbers of those a little better-off, however, made increasing use of these small, horse-drawn vehicles.

Because the individual bus operators needed to run a timetable on each route, associations of formerly competing proprietors were formed on the various roads and a place in the timetable (a 'time') was allocated to each vehicle. Any subsequent intruders were 'nursed': association buses always ran immediately ahead of them and deprived them of fares until they were driven away. The more successful operators could, however, grow by buying times from others in the association, and newcomers could also join them by buying times. Larger businesses began to emerge.

In 1855, when about 800 buses were running in London, some of these larger firms joined a French-promoted company, capitalised at £1m, the London General Omnibus Company (LGOC), which bought out many of their smaller associates and eventually built up a fleet of about 600 vehicles. Most of the remainder which preferred to retain their independence ran in agreement with the new combine. It achieved economies of scale in the purchase and processing of horse feed and in stabling. Further cost reductions occurred after the mid-1870s as the international price of fodder and other purchases fell. Fares were reduced, though still not to levels which wage-earners could regularly afford. Nevertheless, London's bus operators (the LGOC, its associates and some independents – including, from 1882, a new and important one, the London Road Car Company) increased the total bus traffic in the capital from 60 million journeys in 1860 to 300 million in 1896. On London's busiest thoroughfares, four buses were scheduled in each direction *every minute*; and they picked up or set down anywhere along the route (Barker, 1980, *78–81, 84*). Provincial towns did not experience such enviable frequencies, though omnibuses began to run out from them to serve country districts. Privately-owned horse-drawn public transport grew impressively to meet the needs of the growing population.

For those who preferred, and could afford, more private forms of transport, there were other hackney vehicles: coaches which could accommodate several people or families (with or without luggage) and the fleeter two-wheel *cabriolets* (or cabs), another novelty from Paris in the 1820s, which carried two people. Both were improved during the 1830s, the latter (by Hansom among others) to become the standard two-wheeler of Victorian times with the driver sitting at the back, high over his vehicle. The number of cabs and public carriages in London grew from 2650 in the mid-1840s to nearly 11,500 at its peak in 1888 (Barker & Robbins, I, *7, 14, 261*; Georgano, Ch. 1). And while Sherlock Holmes and his like hailed these vehicles, the wealthier owned them or hired them for long periods, together with the horses that went with them, as the mews, coach houses and stables behind the larger dwellings in London and all the growing towns attest.

Horse tramways for all

The horse tramway, introduced to Britain from America, was another important development which did not involve any new method of traction. It is better described by its American name, the street railway, for the use of rails in place of the road surface itself enabled horse-drawn transport to share with the steam railway the advantages of lower rolling resistance (McKay, *13–35*; Miller, Ch. 2). Two horses could pull a larger, heavier vehicle seating 48 passengers instead of 25. Costs were reduced per seat and lower fares made possible. After a false start at the beginning of the 1860s, the horse tramway was successfully introduced to London, Liverpool, Leeds, Hull, Glasgow and other British towns from 1870 using rails laid flush with the road surface so as not to impede other vehicles. For the first time fares were charged which wage earners could afford. Workmen's fares on early morning trams, running usually soon after 5 a.m., cost as little as two old pence a day *return*. The new tramways soon generated much additional traffic as the various systems were extended. Originally built by private capital, on 21-year leases from local authorities for the use of the highways, many were subsequently municipalised (Klapper, Chs 2–4, *8–14*). In most towns they replaced the horse buses on the busiest, central routes; in London, however, the buses held their own because the local authorities kept the tramways out of the City and West End. London's horse trams were nevertheless responsible for 280 million journeys a year by the mid-1890s, almost as many as the horse buses (Barker, *77*). Horse-drawn vehicles were undoubtedly greatly increasing the volume of passenger transport, especially in the growing towns, in the heyday of the Railway Age.

Goods transport

It is more difficult to assess the growth of urban freight transport by road, for this subject has been sadly neglected by historians. It is clear, however, that the volume of goods to be moved increased greatly in response to the country's quickening commercial activity, especially in view of the need to handle the rising volume of foreign trade passing into and out of the ports and other towns.

Even in the big cities animals were still being driven to market on the hoof for much of the nineteenth century, though in London the principal cattle market was moved out of the main built-up area. As traffic on the hoof declined, that of carcases conveyed by vehicle grew. Raw materials and merchandise were also carried in bulk by slow, lumbering waggons from dock or railway goods yard to warehouses and other wholesaling premises in the centre. Mayhew, writing in the middle of the nineteenth century, mainly about retail distribution, presents a vivid picture of London (and perhaps other towns to a smaller extent) as a place constantly on the move with thousands of people carrying loads on their backs, pushing handcarts or wheeling barrows. The more successful owned their own horses, or donkeys, carts, vans or waggons. 'Coal-shed men' supplied the lanes and alleys. More substantial coal merchants moved up market, the most prosperous of them delivering by vehicles 'loaded with sacks standing perpendicularly . . . drawn by four immense horses' (Mayhew, II, *81–9*). The delivery of beer barrels from brewery to public house also accounted for many heavy waggons. So did collection and delivery of rail freight: the railways employed 6000 horses in London alone, according to an estimate made in the early 1890s. They were capable, on occasion, of delivering a huge load weighing 13 tons in a single road vehicle. Other carriers were believed to employ a further 19,000 horses in London at that time (Gordon, *49, 51, 67*). Throughout the country, there was also a vast increase in the movements of mails by road. Fleets of vans carried them from the major railway stations to post offices and between the main offices. After the Post Office started to handle parcels in 1883, these were transferred to road services whenever possible in order to avoid payment to the railway companies: 10 per cent of the new parcel traffic was carried by road at first but this grew in due course (Daunton, *62, 138*). Many illustrations, notably those by Doré, of urban street scenes, show severe urban congestion, with jay-walking pedestrians picking their way through the agglomeration of handcarts and slow-moving horse-drawn goods vehicles of all shapes and sizes, as well as the faster passenger traffic.

We know more about goods transport outside the towns thanks to Everitt's research into carrier services, to which attention has already been drawn. He stresses that 'local traffic on the roads could not have been brought to an end by the railways . . . In the country districts of counties like Kent and Leicestershire, only one village in eight or nine possessed rail communications; in a county like Dorset or Westmorland, it was no doubt fewer . . . Local carriers rapidly increased in numbers and considerably extended the market area of the town. In a sense the railway helped to increase their prosperity because of the growing need for road connections between outlying villages and the railhead.' Market day in a place like Maidstone in the later nineteenth century 'must often have been a solid block of carts and horses from end to end of the town, with 50 carriers parking in the High Street alone, not to mention the crowd of farmers' waggons and tradesmen's vans'. Maidstone was one of the most important market towns; but there were more than 400 others, large and small, throughout the country and, according to Everitt, probably 30,000 or 40,000 carriers all told (Everitt, 1973, *217–18*; 1976, *196*).

He also reminds us of the vast army of workers who were employed in keeping all these horses, carts and waggons on the road. Despite the disintegration of the peasant economy before the nineteenth century, 'many of the old crafts and occupations which had grown up alongside it not only survived but found a new role for themselves in the world of steam power. The wheelwrights and blacksmiths, for instance . . . never flourished more abundantly than during the last decade of Queen Victoria's reign'. In Kent alone there were more than 350 wheelwright's shops and about 600 smiths (Everitt, 1976, *179*; Sturt). The market for horses was well organised and grew. Many more were bred in Britain than before; but little further progress seems to have been made with horse breeding itself, at least until the later nineteenth century (Mingay, *260–8, 351–2*; Trow-Smith, *296–7*).

F. M. L. Thompson has made a courageous, and as yet unchallenged, attempt to estimate the increased volume of road transport in town and country. Using such tax returns as are available, together with other sources, he suggests that the number of commercial road vehicles in Britain, which might have totalled 116,000 in 1811, grew to perhaps 161,000 in 1851, 388,000 in 1881 and 702,000 in 1901. In addition there was, as we have seen, a greatly increased number of omnibuses, hackney coaches and cabs, as well as many privately-owned vehicles. In 1888 the latter included 51,000 larger, two-horse carriages and over 360,000 smaller, one-horse private runabouts (open two-wheel gigs or traps), the greater number of the latter reflecting the continued rise of the professional and other middle classes. To pull this increasing traffic, and to cater for private riding on horseback, Thompson estimates that the number of horses categorised as 'horses not on farms' grew from an estimated 487,000 in 1811 to 535,000 in 1851 and then at a much faster rate, to 1,358,000 in 1891 and 1,766,000 in 1901 (Thompson, *72, 80*). In the early 1890s, perhaps 300,000 of them (approaching a quarter of the total) were at work on the roads of London (Gordon, *113*).

These figures show how impressively road transport grew during the Railway Age, especially in the later nineteenth century, and they also show the concentration of activity in London. The Victorian Age was as much a horse-drawn society as an age of railways. A rich prize awaited anyone who could mechanise shorter-distance road transport as steam railways had mechanised that over longer distances.

The significant pedal cycle

The pedal cycle, with its light but strong tubular frame, spoked wheels and chain drive, was an essential precursor of mechanical traction even though it depended upon human energy to propel it. The earliest low-powered engines were more effective when fitted to these lighter bicycles, tricycles or quadricycles, than to larger and heavier carriages; and the pneumatic tyre, first used on bicycles, was robust enough to support their weight and reduced rolling resistance on ordinary road surfaces. The United Kingdom led the world in pedal cycle development, especially after the arrival of the safety bicycle, with smaller front wheel and diamond frame, in the mid-1880s. Many of the techniques in cycle manufacture (such as standardisation of parts) and cycle marketing (for instance, regular model changes) were to be used subsequently in motor manufacture. Coventry and other towns in the Midlands, the home of cycle manufacture, were to be the places where the motor industry subsequently developed. Indeed, many familiar names in cycling – Rover, Riley, Humber, Triumph – were later to be equally well known on the bonnets of cars. Morris also began his career in cycles. A cycle dealership network was established throughout the country for the best-known *marques*. Cycle races, organised to publicise new models, and a cycling press also pointed the way ahead.

At first, however, cycles were expensive (about £20 each) and only the better-off could afford them. They were a pleasure vehicle, and well-to-do young men banded together in cycling clubs, each often with its club cap and blazer. They brought additional life to the roads; and the Cyclists Touring Club, in its original form dating from 1878, started to approve places to eat or stay and to put up road signs warning of steep hills. All this anticipated the future spread of motor vehicles and motoring associations. The 'bicycle rider', the *Autocar* aptly pointed out in 1895, 'has accustomed the public mind to the sight of wheeled vehicles without horses'.

In the later 1890s much less expensive bicycles began to be sold and a brisk second-hand market grew. Women as well as men, and purchasers of more modest means, began to ride bicycles not just for pleasure but to save time, instead of walking, or expense, instead of going by public transport. For some years the push-bike became the most widespread form of private transport. The swells then lost interest in what many people could now afford and turned to motor cars or motor bicycles, which were more expensive and exclusive (A. E. Harrison; Watson & Gray, *102–40*).

The mechanisation of road transport: by steam, electricity or internal combustion?

The British, world specialists in steam power in general and railway locomotives in particular, were again busily applying steam to road vehicles from the later 1850s. They made heavy traction engines – very noisy, often emitting smoke and even sparks, and very offensive to other road users and frightening to horses. So much so, that in 1865 Parliament passed an Act limiting their speed to four miles per hour in the country and to two miles per hour in built-up areas. Moreover, a man had to walk 60 yards ahead of each snorting monster to warn of its approach and to help horses past. This – and a subsequent Act in 1878 which gave additional powers to local authorities and required the man walking ahead to carry a red flag – did not, however, prevent the spread of these vehicles for heavy haulage. By the 1890s, there were said to be 8000 of them on the roads of England and Wales alone.[22]

There were then also about 800 steam trams – small locomotives each pulling a tramcar – on some of Britain's tramways. They had some success on lines running between towns, such as those of the

South Staffordshire & Birmingham Steam Tramways, formed in 1883 (Klapper, *143*). Steam was, however, soon to be superseded by electricity on fixed routes, though it continued to power heavier vehicles (buses for a time as well as waggons) where manoeuvrability was required (Davison, *26–30*).

Meanwhile, improved technology made possible higher boiler pressures, and therefore a greater power to weight ratio, for steampowered vehicles. Oil, instead of coal, firing was also developed, and some steam tricycles were built in England and France, where, in 1884, Léon Serpollet invented a flash boiler capable of producing sudden bursts of power to give them greater acceleration (Laux, *13–14*). These light, steam-driven runabouts gained some popularity; indeed the French word *chauffeur* (stoker) came to be generally adopted for any paid driver of a mechanically-driven road vehicle. But by the 1890s other sorts of motors were being developed which seemed more promising.

During the 1880s, electricity, starting to spread as a new source of lighting, was also being considered as a form of energy for driving motors. This was relatively straightforward for stationary motors but presented considerable problems with moving vehicles, for they could hardly carry cables round with them. Electricity was, however, a suitable substitute for horse power to drive small and relatively light tramcars running along rails. Some pioneer lines, particularly those built in Northern Ireland and at Blackpool, helped early development, but the real breakthrough came with F. J. Sprague's successful introduction of the overhead trolley to operate many cars at the same time on the hilly horse tramway system at Richmond, Virginia, in 1888. Electric tramways soon spread rapidly elsewhere in the United States but more slowly in Britain, where local authorities waited for the technology to be further developed and, in any case, looked less favourably upon unsightly wires carrying 500 volts suspended over their roads. From the mid-1890s, however, the new, faster and well-lit electric trams spread rapidly within Britain's towns, and sometimes beyond town boundaries out into the country, where they encouraged further building. Replacing the costly horses, they provided not only a better service but also lower fares. Tramway traffic in London grew from 280 million journeys in the mid-1890s to 812 million journeys in 1913–14. Journeys throughout the country,

2.15 million in 1904–5, had reached 3.3 million in 1913–14 (Klapper, *55–64*; Barker, 1980, *77*; Munby, *297*).

Electric traction was not, however, generally successful for use in vehicles which did not follow a regular route, that is to say, for most road vehicles. Batteries were tried, but these, made of lead, were too heavy and had to be recharged too often. Electric vehicles survived the early experimental stage only in a very limited way, for use in shop deliveries and early morning milk rounds where speed was unimportant and quietness a great advantage. For most other road traffic, it was the internal combustion engine which was to replace the horse.

Gas engines, fed by pipe from town gasworks, had been developed as a source of power for stationary engines since the 1860s, and it was not surprising that specialists in their manufacture, like the German Gottlieb Daimler, should try to adapt the engine to drive vehicles, just as the Stephensons and others had contrived to put the steam engine on wheels half a century earlier. The new engines used light fractions of oil, carried in a tank on the vehicle and vaporised easily in transit. The distillation was given various names: gasoline, for instance. In Britain its trade name was petrol.

Experimental work took place in south Germany in the 1880s and, by the mid-1890s, motor tricycles and even horseless carriages were being produced there and in France. They began to attract a few well-to-do young purchasers, especially from Britain, who were prepared to regard keeping them on the road as a sort of sport, and quite a dangerous one at that since they had totally inadequate brakes. When the Red Flag restrictions were removed in November 1896, a few of these young bloods, such as The Hon. C. S. Rolls, took up the new sport, and their numbers soon grew. They enjoyed themselves competing with one another in races or endurance tests. Not infrequently they set off by car but had to return by train after a breakdown or accident. As with the cyclists, they banded together in local clubs for mutual help. The first national organisation, the Automobile Club of Great Britain and Ireland (later the Royal Automobile Club), was formed in 1897. It was followed in 1905 by the Automobile Association, which put on the main roads a corps of pedal cyclists to warn any over-enthusiastic member about police speed traps ahead (Laux, Chs 1–8; Plowden, Ch. 1, *65–6*).

Presenting a fearsome appearance, dressed in leather motoring gear and wearing goggles, these young swells braved all weathers in their open vehicles, though they usually confined their motoring to the summer months. Herbert Austin, who had started to build cars himself, was delighted when, in June 1898, he managed to coax his first Wolseley tricycle the 250 miles from Birmingham to Rhyl and back without a breakdown. In April 1900, 65 tricycles, quadricycles and motor carriages set off from London on a leisurely, 1000-mile trip organised by the Automobile Club to Edinburgh and back. Great satisfaction was expressed when 32 of these still unreliable new-fangled contraptions managed to cover the whole distance under their own power. As there were then still only 1500 petrol-driven vehicles in the whole country – not enough to warrant petrol stations (motorists had to rely on cycle shops and chemists) – the Automobile Club had to make special arrangements to have stocks deposited in cans at regular intervals on the route (Barker, 1987, *35, 39, 45*).

The rapid mechanisation of passenger transport by road, 1904–14

Reliability and quality improved considerably in the years immediately after 1900. Motor bicycles also started to appear on the roads, many of them made in Britain. Registration began in January 1904, by which time ownership was spreading rapidly. In April of that year there were 14,000 cars and 16,000 motor cycles carrying their new number plates, and by September 1905 about 35,000 of each. By then they were being used not only for pleasure but also for business and professional purposes, especially by doctors. Motor cars and bicycles were replacing horses for personal travel at a rapid rate and many people bought them who had never before possessed any transport of their own other than a pedal cycle. The new drivers included women, for whom Dorothy Levett published, in 1909, *The Woman and The Car. A Chatty Little Handbook For All Women Who Motor or Who Want to Motor* ('Indispensable to the motoriste who is going to drive her own car is the overall . . . Never drive the engine downhill'). Garages and petrol supplies, hard to find in 1900, spread rapidly during the

Edwardian period. By 1914 the carriage horse, like the tramway horse, had usually been replaced by motor vehicles in towns, and was increasingly being replaced in country areas too. Hackney coaches and cabs had been largely replaced by motor vehicles equipped with taximeters. They soon came to be called taxis for short (Georgano, Ch. 3).

Traffic censuses taken in London in 1912 revealed that only 13 per cent of all *passengers* riding into the capital came by horse-drawn vehicle, and in 1913 a mere 6 per cent. By then the buses had also been motorised. This had occurred rather fitfully and expensively during the early years of the century but very rapidly indeed after 1908 with the development of a sufficiently robust vehicle capable of repeatedly starting and stopping without being shaken to pieces. As with the electrified tramway, the new, faster motor bus had a greater range, developed longer routes and made possible many more Sunday excursions. It could carry more passengers than the old horse bus and, above all, it was less costly to operate. With greater speed and lower fares the motor bus generated much more traffic, especially in central London where the tramways had never been allowed to penetrate (Barker & Robbins, II, *167–8*).

Outside London motor bus services had also been attempted in Edinburgh and elsewhere from 1898, but usually had a short life. The railway companies started to run them on undemanding, rural routes from 1903 instead of building additional branch lines: the Great Western from Helston to the Lizard in Cornwall, for instance, and the North Eastern between Beverley and Beeford in Yorkshire. Various private concerns, often one-man businesses, started to operate buses in different parts of the country. Municipalities also became interested. Eastbourne, for instance, which had never had its own trams, opted for motor buses in 1903 (Hibbs, *42–68*).

In the later nineteenth century a number of local authorities, including the largest, had acquired the privately-owned gas and electricity undertakings in their areas. Apart from any political views that they might hold about the merits of municipal trading – sometimes rather exaggeratedly described as 'gas and water socialism' – it was logical that they should also take over the private horse tramways, and electrify them. Glasgow, Leeds, Manchester,

Liverpool and Birmingham Corporations were all among those
which started to run municipal electric tramways just before, or
after, 1900. The largest local authority of all, the London County
Council, opened its system south of the river in 1903 and north of
it a few years later. Many of the tramways elsewhere in London
and in other parts of the country, however, remained in private
hands. One particularly large and enterprising business, the British
Electric Traction Co. Ltd (BET), acquired, electrified and developed many of them. It also came to operate its own bus subsidiary.
Exploitation of the new technologies in Britain was both public
and private. The present debate about the merits of public service
and private enterprise in transport has a long history.

The new electric tramways ran on their own rebuilt and
strengthened tracks; but the other increased road traffic required
new road surfaces. Pneumatic tyres, as they spread from bicycles to
motor cars, raised clouds of dust from the existing thoroughfares,
except in towns where wooden blocks or granite setts had already
been laid. In 1902, the County Surveyor of Nottinghamshire
patented a method of mixing bitumen and ironstone slag or stone
to produce a material which sealed the road surface. He christened
it Tarmac and, with others, set up a company to exploit it (Earle,
16–17). Through the automobile clubs, whose members were well
represented on county councils and other road authorities, motorists used their influence to direct more local taxes towards re-
surfacing, until, in the budget of 1909, a graduated horse power
tax and a small petrol duty were introduced to fund a national
Road Fund. This was administered by a Road Board, which
concentrated upon surfacing rather than road improvement. It
later became the Ministry of Transport, formed in 1919.

By the First World War, therefore, Britain had ceased to be a
horse-drawn society so far as most passenger transport was concerned. The coming of the electric motor and the internal combustion engine, however, was intended to replace the horse for short
journeys rather than to compete with the railway for longer ones.
Yet the failure of the railways to share in further traffic growth just
before 1914 suggests that motor vehicles were already beginning to
attract railway passengers over distances which were not quite so
short (Barker, 1986, *332–4*). This competition caused railway
companies to electrify certain lines in the London area, in the

Table 3 *Passenger motor vehicles in use in Britain, 1904–14* (*thousands*)

	Private cars	Motor cycles	Motor buses, coaches & taxis
March			
1904*	8*	*	5*
1905*	16*	*	7*
1906	23		10
1907	32		12
1908	41		15
1909	48		16
1910	53	36	24
1911	72	48	33
1912	88	70	35
1913	106	98	39
1914	132	124	51

Source: B. R. Mitchell, *British Historical Statistics* (Cambridge, 1988), 577.

* The table is based upon the British Road Federation's *Basic Road Statistics* and gives totals for March 1904 and March 1905 which are both much lower than those cited earlier for April 1904 and September 1905, derived from two official sources, a return published in British Parliamentary Papers in 1904 and a Royal Commission Report in 1906. Definition of various sorts of motor vehicle were far from precise at that time and the exclusion from the table above of 4000 and 9000 goods vehicles in those two years provides part of the explanation. It is assumed that the British Road Federation's figures were all calculated on the same basis and can, therefore, be used as a rough indication of traffic growth; but, in order to compile a more reliable set of statistics, some research is required both at local record offices where some of the original registers are kept, and among the records at the PRO.

North East and in Lancashire in and after 1904. When motor buses appeared in greater numbers a few years later, they probably won much traffic which would otherwise have gone by train. In general, however, road and rail were still complementary. Road transport, now mechanised for short passenger journeys, had become more efficient and cheaper in much the same way as medium and longer distance transport had been made more efficient and cheaper by the steam railway 50 and more years before.

Although tramway statistics have enabled us to show a 50 per cent growth in traffic between 1904–5 and 1913–14, no comparable figures were collected which enable us to quantify the effects of the internal combustion engine on the growth of passenger traffic. Although returns of the numbers of vehicles in use enable us to give an indication of this (Table 3), even here the readily available figures are far from satisfying, for totals relating to taxis have been aggregated with those of buses and coaches. In interpreting these totals, it should be remembered that a double-deck motor bus could seat 35 passengers, compared with a maximum of 25 in a horse bus; and because it could travel at twice the speed, the motor bus could also do twice the work. Its lower working costs, like those of the electric tramcar, made it possible to reduce fares and therefore attract the traffic needed to fill more of the larger number of seats.

The more gradual mechanisation of goods transport by road

The substitution of motors for horses occurred much more slowly in freight transport. In 1913, when hardly any horse-drawn passenger vehicles were entering London, the traffic census still recorded 88 per cent of the goods vehicles as horse-drawn. Indeed, according to Thompson, the number of horses used in freight transport actually rose between 1901 and 1911, from 702,000 to 832,000. There was not the same incentive to invest more fixed capital in goods vehicles, which were kept standing about for much of the time; nor was greater speed an advantage unless rapid delivery was required, and it is motor delivery vans we hear most about in the early years of the century. They probably accounted for most of the 85,000 motorised goods vehicles registered in 1914 – far less numerous than the 307,000 cars, motor cycles, buses and taxis.

Technical reasons also contributed to the slower mechanisation of freight vehicles. It was more difficult to power these heavier vehicles. This was evident from trials carried out in and around Liverpool in 1898, 1899 and 1901 in an attempt to break the railway's control of freight rates between Liverpool and Manchester. None of the various types of motor lorry then tried was reliable enough for commercial use without further development, though steam put up the most promising showing. Edmund

Shrapnell-Smith, who organised these trials, wrote a few years later that, while petrol motors predominated in the motorised carriage of freight up to two tons, steam waggons shared with petrol motors the carriage of heavier loads (Barker, 1986, *331–2*). The steam waggon was to be a familiar sight on Britain's roads until the Second World War. The steam bus was also able to survive petrol bus competition on a few routes until the end of the First World War.

It was fortunate that road passenger and freight transport were not mechanised simultaneously. If that had happened, a whole industry based on horse haulage, which greatly expanded during the nineteenth century, would have been suddenly swept away: not only the actual operation of the passenger and freight vehicles but also all the associated businesses to which we have already referred: horse breeding, the supply of fodder and harness, and the care and stabling of the horses. Many people directly or indirectly connected with horse transport would have been thrown out of work – much as the swollen force of handloom weavers had been made redundant by new machinery in cotton over half a century before. As we have just noted, horse-drawn freight transport actually grew during the critical decade after 1904 when it was falling on the passenger side. Some of the drivers moved to the new motors; but what we now call natural wastage – not filling the jobs of those who retired or left the industry for some other reason – seems to have taken care of the situation. The horse men despised the new, oily, noisy and inanimate motors and would have nothing to do with them. They left them to a new generation who were keen on machinery and technical progress. There were enough jobs left for those who preferred horses as the industry ran down, with nearly as many horses in freight transport in 1924 (374,000) as there had been, according to Thompson's estimate, in 1881. When the fifth census of freight transport horses was taken in 1934, the total had fallen to 131,000 (Thompson, *64*). Some horse-drawn carts and waggons were still to be seen on Britain's roads in the years immediately after 1945; indeed a few continue to be used even now.

Part 4

Motor transport between the wars

The motor vehicle, having replaced the horse in passenger transport, captures almost all the horse-drawn freight traffic and much that would otherwise have gone by goods train.

The total number of registered motor goods vehicles, which had fallen to 41,000 in 1918, reached 100,000 in 1920, considerably more than in 1914. Army purchases had encouraged lorry manufacture during the war. After it, many ex-servicemen bought these vehicles, sold cheaply as army surplus, and set up one-man businesses; and, as the vehicle manufacturers returned to the civilian market, more commercial vehicles of all sorts came onto the roads. More central and local government expenditure was devoted to the building of new roads and the improvement of older ones. The vehicles which ran upon them were also improved year by year. Solid tyres were replaced by pneumatics on these heavier vehicles in the 1920s; diesel engines, greatly improved, enjoyed more popularity in the 1930s; better braking systems came into use. There were still, however, about 9000 steam freight vehicles on the roads in the later 1920s. Either as steam tractors pulling up to three trailers each, or as steam waggons, almost all of four tons or more unladen weight, they carried the heaviest loads (Brunner, 35–7). With the improved efficiency of larger motor vehicles, articulated or rigid (including some eight-wheelers from 1930), steam waggons lost favour. Only about 1000 of them remained in 1938.

The nominal speed limit of 20 miles per hour for heavier lorries was often exceeded and there was much overloading. As someone who knew the industry well has explained: 'The normal procedure was to buy a $2\frac{1}{2}$ tonner in whatever condition could be afforded, then double its capacity overnight by just calling it a five-tonner. Then it was loaded with $7\frac{1}{2}$ tons of payload but driven considerately so that its back was not broken' (Tuck, 5–6).

The number of commercial vehicles grew to 350,000 in 1930 and nearly 500,000 in 1938; but of these 500,000, 220,000 were car-based delivery vans or runabouts of under $1\frac{1}{2}$ tons unladen. About the same number, weighing between $1\frac{1}{2}$ and $2\frac{1}{2}$ tons unladen, constituted the vast majority of lorries. There remained only 40,000 between $2\frac{1}{2}$ and 4 tons unladen and a further 22,000 over four tons. In view of the amount of overloading, it is impossible even to begin to guess the increase in ton mileage carried by road between 1920 and 1938; but the best estimate of mileage alone suggests that *all* commercial vehicles, both above and below $1\frac{1}{2}$ tons unladen, may have covered 2400 million miles in the early 1920s and 8000 million miles in 1938 (Armitage, 4).

Most of this increased traffic by road was carried over short distances and did not compete with that by railway; but in the 1920s more motor vehicles were able to make round trips of 120 miles or so in a day, direct from door to door. Firms like Sainsbury's which previously had to crate goods destined for their more distant branches and have them carried to and from the railway at each end, could now dispatch them all the way, uncrated, in their own motor vans.[23] Building materials, a growing traffic as the housing boom developed, could also go direct from source to building site. Produce could be brought direct from farm to market. Road hauliers concentrated upon particular traffics over medium distances while the railways, obliged as common carriers to accept any goods offered to them, were left with the rest.

Commercial vehicles became subject to regulation by the Road and Rail Traffic Act, 1933. They had to be kept in a fit and serviceable condition and their drivers were forbidden to drive continuously for more than a specified number of hours. Log books had to be kept. (As with overloading and speed limits, there is much evidence of the flouting of the law; but at least a start had been made.) Licences, issued by Area Traffic Commissioners, divided owners into three categories. The most numerous, holders of 'C' licences, were private businesses, like Sainsbury's, which carried their own goods. Applicants for 'A' and 'B' licenses – general hauliers and private businesses which also undertook general haulage work – were obliged to satisfy their local Area Traffic Commissioners that 'suitable transport facilities' were not already available. Their applications for licences were open to objection by railway companies or others, and the Commissioners' verdict was open to appeal.

Most hauliers were small operators with low overheads. In 1938, for instance, there were nearly 27,000 'A' licence and 34,000 'B' licence holders in possession of 93,000 and 54,000 vehicles respectively. When the few and quite exceptional large road haulage concerns, like Pickford's, with 46 motors in 1919 and 628 in 1933, are taken into account, this works out at very few vehicles – often only one – per operator. Most vehicles (365,000) were run by the 178,000 private 'C' licence concerns. The more ambitious hauliers started with a single vehicle but were prepared to expand their businesses, buying more lorries and hiring other drivers. Then, in due course, they gave up driving themselves and stayed at base to deal with customers and general management tasks – more often than not previously undertaken by their wives when they themselves were away on the road. A good example of such a firm is that of John Jempson & Son, whose business records have been studied.

John Jempson, the founder, started his business at Rye, near Hastings, with a Model 'T' Ford light lorry which he bought for £124 in 1924. A few years later he was able to acquire a Thornycroft for £800 and an ex-First World War Packard, each of which was supposed to carry not more than four tons but was invariably overloaded. At first most of his business was local; but then he began to carry fruit and agricultural produce the 60 miles to London. Setting off early in the morning, he could deliver his load to the appropriate market and, later the same day, bring back fertiliser, flour or cattle food from the London docks. Soon afterwards the main part of his business consisted of the transport of bricks from Ore, not far from Rye, or concrete pipes, manhole covers or kerbs, made at Rye itself, to building sites in the rapidly growing London suburbs, even as far as Kenton in North London. He did not have to undercut the railway on costs or even to visit the local station to discover the railway rates; his customers told him what they were. His service was quicker and more reliable, with a single loading and unloading. Customers willingly paid him the railway rate. Any cost cutting that there may have been resulted from competition by other road hauliers (Barker, 1982, *17–39*). Motor vehicles had no difficulty in capturing all this profitable traffic, which would otherwise have gone by rail, even with relatively undeveloped vehicles running along winding roads. In the winter months there was much running in the dark, with paraffin lamps as the sole means of illuminating the road ahead. Gilbert Walker estimated that in 1924 road transport conveyed 13,600 tons of merchandise which would otherwise have gone by rail; by 1935 this total had grown to 50,000 tons. (The total in those merchandise categories actually carried by rail in these years fell from 61,000 to 45,000 tons (Walker, *123*).)

The growing importance of the motor bus

Road passenger traffic also grew impressively between the wars. Motor buses, like motor lorries, were much improved technically during the 1920s, and the heaviest of them started to run on pneumatic, instead of solid rubber, tyres by the end of the decade, by which time there were some 70-seat double deckers in service. They carried many more people at lower cost and in greater comfort, with covered decks for those travelling on top. Bus routes in town and country ran much closer than railways to people's homes and saved journeys to and from the nearest railway station.

Local authority buses outside London were originally used to supplement their electric trams. They carried only about 24 million passengers in the year 1918–19 but this total had reached about 482 million by 1927–28, in which years London's buses, favoured, as we have seen, because trams were kept out of the centre, were carrying 729 million and 1834 million respectively (Munby, *302–3*; Barker & Robbins, II, *215*). To these journeys need to be added those on bus services run in their distinctive colours by private companies outside London and the main provincial towns, many of them owned by a few relatively large concerns developed immediately after the war to serve particular areas. Some grew out of ventures pioneered by able entrepreneurs such as Edward Crosland-Taylor (Crosville); others, for example Midland Red, were owned or supported (often in collaboration with Tilling) by the British Electric Traction Co. Ltd (Hibbs, Ch. 4). These provincial businesses carried twice the London total in 1930–31 when their statistics were first collected. If we estimate their journeys at 3500 million in 1927–28, the grand total in that year was already of the order of 5800 million. This was already considerably more than the 4140 million journeys on all Britain's tramways in that year, their peak. The decade after 1918, that is to say, saw the most rapid growth of motor bus traffic both in London and elsewhere in Britain (Klapper; Barker & Robbins; Munby).

Motor bus traffic continued to grow in the 1930s, but much more slowly, subject to regulation by Traffic Commissioners appointed under the Road Traffic Act 1930 (Glaister & Mulley, Chs 3 and 4). In 1937–38, the last pre-war year for which we have statistics, the total number of bus journeys had grown by only another 800 million or so to 6664 million (over 2000 million of which were in the London area, under the control of the London Passenger Transport Board from 1933). Tramway traffic, however, had by then fallen to 3262 million journeys; but an additional 700 million journeys were accounted for by that hybrid, the trolley bus, first seen in service in Britain, in Bradford and Leeds, in 1911 and taken up extensively in the London area from 1931 (Owen, *23, 66*; Munby, *298, 303, 537*).

The widespread effects in town and country of this vast increase in public passenger transport by road should not be underestimated. To a large extent town dwellers had already experienced by 1914 the benefits of mechanisation, by electric tramways and, in London's special case, by motor buses. Most country motor bus services and services between towns, however, did not appear until after 1918. Country dwellers, dependent on carriers' carts in horse-drawn days, were now enabled to ride more frequently, quickly and cheaply into the nearest towns where shopping was more competitive and a wider choice of goods available. They had time to do this themselves instead of entrusting it to carriers. Audiences at the new cinemas often depended on buses to get them there and back. Schoolchildren were no longer so reliant on local, single-teacher schools, being able to travel to larger schools farther away where more specialised teaching was available. Townsmen did not have to rely solely upon excursion trains if they wanted to get out into the country at weekends or on Bank Holidays.

It needs to be emphasised that the tram and bus were in these years bestowing the benefits of the new technologies upon the public at large, not just the privileged minority who could afford their own cars or motor cycles. Only 187,000 cars and 288,000 motor cycles were registered in 1920 and just over a million cars and 724,000 motor cycles ten years later. The sale of cheaper, small saloon models in the early 1930s increased the motor car's popularity while that of motor cycles declined. Even so, only just over 2 million cars were registered in August 1939 and 418,000 motor cycles. Earnings were still such that only the middle classes could afford to run them, though better-off artisan wage-earners owned motor cycles, sometimes with pillion riders and often with sidecars attached in which their wives and children were carried. Many of these private cars and motor cycles were still used mainly for pleasure and were licensed only for the summer months. Journeys to work, even by the better-off, were still usually made on foot, by pedal cycle or by public transport.

The vast increase in passenger journeys by road – by bus and tram rather than by car or motor bicycle – deprived the railways of much of their shorter-distance passenger traffic. The number of journeys by train fell from 1749 million in 1922 (after the post-war boom) to 1236 million in 1938. However, as most people continued to use the train for medium and longer distances, the total of passenger miles travelled by rail remained about the same at the two dates: 20,000 million; but the railways had been obliged to cut fares to hold this traffic, and their income from passengers fell from £83 million in 1922 to £59 million in 1938 (Munby, *101, 104, 109*).

Part 5
The motorway age

The carriage of goods

Commercial motor transport, having by 1938 almost completely replaced horse-drawn traffic and deprived the railways of most of their merchandise freight over distances of up to 60 miles or so, proceeded to gain goods traffic over longer distances after 1945. As Table 4 shows, the number of delivery vans and runabouts under $1\frac{1}{2}$ tons grew impressively. So, too, did the number of lorries over three tons, the trend being towards fewer but larger vehicles. And their payloads increased more than proportionately: a five-tonner, for instance, was allowed by law to carry 11 tons, and an eight-tonner, 16 tons. After 1965, the grand total grew much more slowly; but within that total the larger vehicles went on increasing fast, especially the largest of them (over eight tons unladen). The permitted *gross* weight limits were raised for four-axle vehicles: to 24 tons in 1955, to 32 tons in 1964 (articulated) and 30 tons in 1972 (rigid), and to 38 tonnes in 1983 (1 ton (UK)=1.016 metric tonnes).

These larger and technically improved vehicles did more work per day by running at higher speeds on better roads. More dual carriageways were constructed and, from 1959, when the first part of the M1 was opened from the northern suburbs of London to a point near Rugby, a purpose-built motorway network was created over which this increasing number of juggernauts thundered, at 70 miles per hour or more whatever their legal speed limit may have been. No longer was 120 miles the maximum daily return distance. Confronted by such greatly increased competition, even coastal

Table 4 *Goods vehicles by unladen weight, 1948–79 (thousands)*

	1946	1950	1955	1960	1965	1970	1975	1979
Under 1½ tons	204	364	534	757	864	933	1107	1153
1½–3 tons	279	401	407	348	269	197	204	167
3–5 tons	37	65	93	186	269	234	162	142
5–8 tons	10	15	26	41	76	132	134	114
Over 8 tons	1	2	5	11	24	55	96	121
Total	530	847	1064	1342	1502	1552	1703	1697

Source: Armitage, 5.

shipping lost traffic to the roads. The railways, now facing competition over longer distances, found themselves in a much worse plight.

The Labour government had originally intended to nationalise both road and rail by its Transport Act of 1947. The four railway companies and all the services of the London Passenger Transport Board came under public control but private businesses which carried their own goods and held C licences were excluded. Only 42,000 A- and B-licensed vehicles were nationalised and all but 10,000 of these, which became the property of British Road Services (BRS) companies, were returned to private ownership between 1954 and 1956 by the subsequent Conservative government, often to the considerable financial advantage of the recipients (Barker, 1982, *43–6*).

Smaller businesses still preponderated, though there were more larger-sized units after denationalisation than there had been before. The nationalised railways, in an attempt to hold their freight traffic against the growing onslaught, produced in 1955 a Modernisation Plan which, *inter alia*, entailed the rather tardy universal adoption of the new technologies of electric and diesel traction in place of steam, and a drastic reorganisation of freight services. The Plan was never fully implemented. The volume of freight carried by road went on growing impressively, while that by rail continued to fall.

The effect of larger vehicles and motorways is clear from road transport's vast growth after 1956. With water transport no longer important and rail freight transport in decline, the nation

Table 5 *Ton-miles of freight, 1952–90 (thousand millions)*

	Road	Rail	Total
1952	19.0	22.6	53.8
1956	23.2	21.4	58.1
1960	30.0	18.3	61.2
1964	40.4	15.9	72.2
1968	48.3	14.1	78.9
1972	53.8	12.8	83.2
1976	58.7	12.8	90.5
1980	56.5	10.8	106.5
1984	61.1	7.8	111.7
1988	79.6	11.1	133.8
1990	83.3	9.7	131.8

Total includes carriage by water and pipeline.
Note: 1 ton-mile=1.635 tonne-kilometres.
Source: Department of Transport, *Transport Statistics Great Britain 1991* (1991), tables 7.3, 1.13.

depended upon road transport more than ever before for the movement of freight.

The advantages of road transport's greater speed and versatility need further emphasis. At greater speeds drivers could cover far longer distances in a given stint. Lower stocks could be kept by customers with savings in working capital. Vehicles could be unloaded and repacked at modern, computerised transfer points in a surprisingly short time. Some of the largest hauliers now have their own transfer points. So, too, do the supermarkets. Suppliers deliver goods in their own vehicles to regional supermarket centres during the day. There these deliveries are distributed into separate lots to be collected at night by the supermarket's (or it's contractor's) own large lorries, one per supermarket, each of which delivers to the particular store first thing the next morning the order it sent in to the distribution centre the previous day. Supermarkets depend not only on this sophisticated, carefully organised lorry system for their supplies but also, more often than not, upon their customers coming in their own motor cars to collect their purchases. The whole population nowadays depends much more upon the road carriage of goods than is often realised.

The rise of private, and the decline of public, transport by road

The remarkable increase in car registrations, from 2 million, the 1939 total regained in 1950, to nearly 20 million in 1990, is the most visible and remarked upon feature of post-war road transport development. (Motor cycle ownership grew much less impressively, from over half a million in 1947 to a peak of 1.74 million in 1960, declining thereafter.) It is as if the private carriage, the exclusive sign of privilege in horse-drawn days, became almost universal as most wage- as well as salary-earning families could afford a car of their own. In 1989, 66 per cent of households had a car and 22 per cent had more than one. Table 6 shows the immense growth of passenger mileage. The roads of Britain were used as never before for personal travel as well as for business and other purposes.

There were still many people, however – the young, the old (even in car-owning families), the poor, and those who, for one reason or another, preferred not to drive – who did not benefit much, if at all, from the spread of car ownership. Indeed, they positively suffered, for public transport by road, which had brought greater mobility for all between the wars, could not withstand the new motor car competition and, as Table 6 shows, went into decline. And the millions of extra cars, together with the increasing commercial traffic already discussed, soon did not have enough road space to run freely at busy times of day, especially in urban centres. Even some of the motorways began to be overloaded. All these additional vehicles, moreover, caused more atmospheric and noise pollution; and more accidents.

Apart from the new motor car competition, the continuation of pre-war trends also brought change in public transport. The switch from tram to bus (though not to trolleybus) continued after 1945. Manchester closed its last tram route in 1949; London in 1952. The total number of tramcars in use in Britain, 14,400 at the peak in 1927, 9000 in 1938 and 6000 at the end of the war, was down to 2000 by 1956. By the early 1960s the only trams to be seen outside museums were running in Blackpool. The trolleybus did not survive much longer: the last in Britain was withdrawn from service in 1972. Other countries often kept, and improved, their

Table 6 *Passenger-miles by mode of transport, 1952–90 (thousand millions)*

	Buses & coaches	Cars, taxis & motor cycles	Pedal cycles	Rail*	All modes
1952	50.3	33.6	14.3	24.2	122.4
1956	48.5	52.2	9.9	24.9	135.5
1960	42.9	78.9	7.5	24.9	154.7
1964	38.5	131.1	5.0	23.0	198.8
1968	34.8	170.9	3.1	21.1	231.2
1972	31.7	202.6	2.5	21.7	259.1
1976	32.9	215.0	3.1	20.5	272.8
1980	28.0	250.4	3.1	21.7	305.1
1984	26.1	275.3	3.7	21.7	328.7
1988	25.5	326.8	3.1	25.5	384.0
1990	25.5	352.9	3.1	25.5	410.1

Source: Department of Transport, *Transport Statistics Great Britain 1991* (1991), tables 7.1, 1.1.
* Includes London Underground, Strathclyde's urban rail system and the Tyne and Wear Metro.

trams and trolleybuses. They may have been wise to retain the former, since the street railway still has advantages in modern, pedestrianised cities, and in the early 1990s the electric tram in its most up-to-date light railway version is being reintroduced into some British cities, the first being Manchester in 1992.

The buses, in their turn, suffered from motor car competition through loss of traffic and vastly increased urban congestion. Bus operators, deprived of traffic, cut their services and caused many townspeople, increasingly impatient at unreliable timekeeping and having to wait longer at stops, to use their own cars. On the fringes of towns or out in the country many were obliged to buy cars who would otherwise have preferred to travel by public transport. The buses were further deprived of traffic by the growing popularity of television, which reduced off-peak evening travel from the mid-1950s, and by the spread of the five-day week, which, from about 1960, began to reduce the number of journeys to work on Saturdays. From a peak of about 13,500 million bus and coach journeys per year in the mid-1950s (when the buses were taking over from the trams), the total fell to under 12,000 million in 1964 and then, more steeply, to just over 9110 million in 1970. The slide continued. In 1988–89 only 5810 bus and coach journeys were taken in Britain. Passenger mileage did not fall so sharply (Table 6). It was the shorter journeys by bus which suffered most; and longer journeys by coach increased in the 1980s after long-distance coaches, often using the motorways, were allowed to compete freely with the railways.

The railways were, however, more successful in retaining their passenger than their goods traffic. Although the number of journeys by rail (including commuters using season tickets) fell from just over a thousand million in 1948 to 760 million in 1980 and 744 million in 1989, in terms of passenger-miles the main-line total held up relatively well: 21,000 million in 1948, 19,000 million in 1980 and 21,000 million in 1989. But by 1990 private and public transport by road accounted for 93 per cent of Britain's passenger miles and the railways for only 6 per cent. (The remaining one per cent was by air.)

Road transport, more important than ever in the 1990s, was always the most important transport mode

Seen with hindsight, the main effect of mechanised road transport came only after 1950. Developments earlier in the twentieth century, though noteworthy – and as regards the spread of trams and buses socially important – were of limited significance when compared with the enormous expansion of the past 40 years.

All history is present-minded in the sense that present events cause us to think more about their antecedents. Our present dependence upon road transport has given us reason to look back to see that, even in 1700, and probably long before then, road transport was much more important than used to be supposed, even though it then shared some of its importance with transport by river and coastal shipping. It went on growing, though it concentrated on traffic over shorter distances after the coming of railways. When road transport itself was mechanised there was little inland water transport left; and such coastal trade as remained was vulnerable to the increasingly efficient motor transport competition. In its more intense form after 1950, it resulted in many railway lines being closed, especially during the Beeching era of the early 1960s. The rest of the railway system survived either because, though loss-making, it merited public support to keep it open on social grounds; or because city centre to city centre more modern trains, which provided faster journeys than road (and air over most British distances), could still be full and profitable; or because railways provided their own, valuable roads into conurbations where the existing thoroughfares were becoming overloaded, particularly at certain times of day.

Government forecasts, which in the past have consistently underestimated the eventual totals, indicate that the rapid growth of road transport will continue. The present forecast is that vehicle-miles will increase between 1990 and 2025 by from 72 to 121 per cent. The uncertainty of travel times by road because of slow-downs and traffic jams shows that we are already running out of road space, especially in towns, despite traffic engineering (one-way streets, timed traffic lights etc.) and such road widening as is possible. That the motor vehicle may need deterring is increasingly being recognised by the pedestrianisation of urban shopping streets. There are powerful arguments for carrying more people in fewer, larger vehicles which, when well patronised, make better use of existing road space and create less air and noise pollution than cars per person carried. This, in its turn, presupposes that the sophisticated forms of electronic road pricing now being developed should be used to deter private motorists and commercial vehicle owners from using their cars, vans and lorries on busy urban roads at certain times of day unless their particular journey is so necessary that they are prepared to pay for it. The resulting decongested roads would then be available for a frequent and more comfortable generation of buses of various sizes to be run at speed and to time. Perhaps light railways (not the tramways of old) might be run through the streets, linking the main suburban railways, as in Manchester.

Are the numbers of vehicles on some of Britain's roads, especially in towns and cities, already reaching their ultimate limit?

Notes

1. Olive Coleman (ed.), *The Brokerage Book of Southampton 1443–1444*, Southampton Record Series IV & VI (1960–61).
2. Peter Mathias, *The First Industrial Nation* (2nd edn, 1983), 104.
3. Thomas De Laune, *The Present State of London* (1681); ibid., *Angliae Metropolis: or, the Present State of London* (1690).
4. John Taylor, *Carriers Cosmographie* (1637).
5. PRO, C 5/244/9; PRO, C 7/237/28; PRO, C 8/556/7; PRO, C 11/1189/64.
6. *Second Report from the Select Committee on Postage* Parliamentary Papers 1837–38 (658) XX, Part II, QQ. 7226, 7236–7.
7. Joseph Nicholson and Richard Burn, *The History and Antiquities of the Counties of Westmorland and Cumberland* (1777), I, 66.
8. Daniel Defoe, *Tour through the Whole Island of Great Britain* (1962 edn), 206–7.
9. J. Aikin, *A Description of the Country from Thirty to Forty Miles round Manchester* (1795), 183–4.
10. Aikin, *Description*, 205.
11. J. U. Nef, *The Rise of the British Coal Industry* (1966), 103.
12. William Marshall, *The Rural Economy of the Midland Counties* (1790), Vol. 1, 307, 309.
13. PRO, C 11/1189/64; PRO, C 112/70, No. 125.
14. *Sherborne Mercury*, 10 May 1737, 21 June 1737, 19 July 1737.
15. *Report from Select Committee on Conveyance and Porterage of Parcels* (Parliamentary Papers 1825 (498) V 255).
16. P. G. Hughes, *Wales and the Drovers* (1943), 49.
17. G. R. Hawke, *Railways and Economic Growth in England and Wales 1840–1870* (1970), 145–6.
18. B. R. Mitchell and Phyllis Deane, *Abstract of British Historical Statistics* (1962), 354.
19. De Laune, *Angliae Metropolis*.
20. PRO, E 112/598/541; see also Gerhold, forthcoming (b).

21. PRO, E 112/598/541; Institution of Civil Engineers, *Minutes of Proceedings*, Vol. 2 (1842–3), 115.
22. *Select Committee on Traction Engines on Roads* (Parliamentary Papers, 1896 (272) XIV), QQ. 224, 238, 241.
23. *J.S. 100: the Story of Sainsbury's* (J. Sainsbury, 1969), 48–50.

Bibliography

Albert, William (1972) *The Turnpike Road System in England 1663–1840*.

Aldcroft, Derek H. (1975) *British Transport since 1914*.

Aldcroft, Derek and Michael Freeman (eds) (1983) *Transport in the Industrial Revolution*. Includes a valuable introduction by Freeman and articles by William Albert on turnpike trusts and by J. A. Chartres and G. L. Turnbull on road transport.

Armitage, Arthur (chairman) (1980) *Inquiry into Lorries, People and the Environment*.

Ashton, T. S. (1939) *An Eighteenth Century Industrialist: Peter Stubs of Warrington, 1756–1806*. Includes a chapter on Stubs's use of carriers by road and water.

Austen, Brian (1981) 'The Impact of the Mail Coach on Public Coach Services in England and Wales, 1784–1840', *Journal of Transport History*, 3rd ser., II, pp. 25–37.

Bagwell, Philip S. (1981) 'The Decline of Rural Isolation' in G. E. Mingay (ed.), *The Victorian Countryside*, I. Only 11 pages of text but full of excellent examples. A gem of clarity and compression, containing all the relevant arguments. It does full justice to the belated influence of rail, as well as to the continued importance of road, transport.

Bagwell, Philip S. (1974) *The Transport Revolution from 1770*; republished as *The Transport Revolution* (1988). (References are to the 1974 edition.)

Barker, T. C. (1980) 'Towards an Historical Classification of Urban Transport Development since the Later Eighteenth Century', *Journal of Transport History*, 3rd ser., I.

Barker, T. C. (1982) *The Transport Contractors of Rye: John Jempson & Son*.

Barker, T. C. (1986) 'Some Thoughts on the Railways' Competitors in General and Road Transport in Particular', *Journal of the Railway & Canal Historical Society*, XXVII, No. 8.

Barker, T. C. (Theo) (ed.) (1987) *The Economic and Social Effects of the Spread of Motor Vehicles.*

Barker, T. C. and Michael Robbins (1963; 1964) *A History of London Transport*, Vol. I; Vol. II.

Barker, T. C. and C. I. Savage (1974) *An Economic History of Transport in Britain.* Christopher Savage's sudden death in 1969, at the age of 44, robbed the academic world of a distinguished scholar. The first five chapters of the book he wrote (first published in 1959), dealing with the roads to 1914, were almost completely new in the 1974 edition.

Barker, T. C. and F. M. L. Thompson (1990) 'Complementary and Competing Technologies: Road Transport before the Motor', in Ferenc Glatz, *Modern Age – Modern Historian* (Budapest).

Bonser, K. J. (1970) *The Drovers.*

Bovill, E. W. (1959) *The England of Nimrod and Surtees 1815–1854.* A useful and vivid introduction to the golden age of stage coaches.

Boyes, Grahame (ed.) (1991) *Preliminary Bibliography of the History of Roads and Road Transport from the Medieval Period up to about 1900* (Railway & Canal Historical Society, 7 Onslow Road, Richmond, Surrey TW10 6QH).

Brunner, Christopher T. (1928) *The Problem of Motor Transport: An Economic Analysis.*

Carlson, Robert E. (1969) *The Liverpool and Manchester Railway Project, 1821–1831.*

Chartres, J. A. in G. E. Mingay (ed.) (1989) *The Agrarian History of England and Wales*, VI, *1750–1850.*

Chartres, J. A. (1977) 'Road Carrying in England in the Seventeenth Century: Myth and Reality', *Economic History Review*, 2nd ser., XXX, pp. 73–94.

Chartres, J. A. (1985) 'The Marketing of Agricultural Produce', in Joan Thirsk (ed.), *The Agrarian History of England and Wales*, V. II, pp. 406-502.

Chartres, J. A. (1989) 'Road Transport and Economic Growth in the 18th Century', *ReFRESH*, 8 (Economic History Society), pp. 5–8. A summary of recent research.

Chartres, J. A. and G. L. Turnbull (1975) *A Pilot Study of Source Materials for an Economic History of British Inland Transport and Communications 1600–1850* (Social Science Research Council).

Chivers, Keith (1976) *The Shire Horse: A History of the Breed, the Society and the Men.*

Colyer, Richard J. (1976) *The Welsh Cattle Drovers: Agriculture and the Welsh Cattle Trade before and during the Nineteenth Century.*

Commercial Motor I No. 7 (27 April 1905), pp. 154–6; XVI No. 414 (13 Feb. 1913), pp. 518–19.

Copeland, J. (1968) *Roads and their Traffic, 1750–1850*.

Daunton, M. J. (1985) *The Royal Mail*.

Davison, C. B. St. C. B. (1953) *History of Steam Motor Vehicles*.

Department of Transport (1991) *Transport Statistics Great Britain 1991*.

Dickinson, G. C. (1959) 'Stage-Coach Services in the West Riding of Yorkshire Between 1830 and 1840', *Journal of Transport History*, IV, pp. 1–12.

Dyos, H. J. and D. H. Aldcroft (1969) *British Transport: an Economic Survey from the Seventeenth Century to the Twentieth*. (References are to the 1974 edition.)

Earle, J. B. F. (1971) *A Century of Road Materials*.

Everitt, Alan (1973) 'Town and Country in Victorian Leicestershire: The Role of the Village Carrier', in Everitt (ed.), *Perspectives in English Urban History*.

Everitt, Alan (1976) 'Country Carriers in the Nineteenth Century', *Journal of Transport History*, 2nd ser., III, pp. 179–202.

Fenelon, K. G. (1925) *The Economics of Road Transport*.

Flink, James J. (1988) *The Automobile Age*.

Freeman, M. J. (1975) 'The Stage-Coach System of South Hampshire, 1775–1851', *Journal of Historical Geography*, I, pp. 259–81.

Freeman, M. J. (1977) 'The Carrier System of South Hampshire, 1775–1851', *Journal of Transport History*, 2nd ser., IV, pp. 61–85.

Freeman, M. J. (1979) 'Turnpikes and their Traffic: the Example of Southern Hampshire', *Institute of British Geographers, Transactions*, new ser., IV, pp. 411–34.

Freeman, M. J. (1982) *A Perspective on the Geography of English Internal Trade During the Industrial Revolution: The Trading Economy of the Textile District of the Yorkshire West Riding Circa 1800* (School of Geography, Oxford, Research Paper 29), pp. 34–45.

Freeman, Michael (1980) 'Transporting Methods in the British Cotton Industry during the Industrial Revolution', *Journal of Transport History*, 3rd ser., I, pp. 59–74.

Freeman, Michael J. and Derek H. Aldcroft (eds) (1988) *Transport in Victorian Britain*.

Fussell, G. E. and Constance Goodman (1937) 'Eighteenth-century traffic in livestock', *Economic History*, III, pp. 214–36.

Georgano, G. N. (1972) *A History of the London Taxicab*.

Gerhold, Dorian (1988) 'The Growth of the London Carrying Trade, 1681–1838', *Economic History Review*, XLI, pp. 392–410.

Gerhold, Dorian (1993) *Road Transport in England before the Railways: Russell's London Flying Waggons*.

Gerhold, Dorian (1993) 'Packhorses and Wheeled Vehicles in England, 1550–1800', *Journal of Transport History*, 3rd ser., XIV.

Gerhold, Dorian (forthcoming, a) 'The Impact of Turnpikes on Road Services'.

Gerhold, Dorian (forthcoming, b) *Carriers and Coachmen of the late Seventeenth Century*.

Ginarlis, J. E. and Sidney Pollard (1988) 'Roads and Waterways 1750–1850', in Charles H. Feinstein and Sidney Pollard (eds), *Studies in Capital Formation in the United Kingdom, 1750–1820*, pp. 182–224.

Glaister, Stephen and Corinne Mulley (1983) *Public Control of the British Bus Industry*.

Gloucestershire Community Council (1950) *I Remember. Travel and Transport in Gloucestershire Villages, 1850–1950*.

Gordon, W. J. (1983) *The Horse World of London*.

Greening, Alan (1971) 'Nineteenth Century Country Carriers in North Wiltshire', *Wiltshire Archaeological and Natural History Magazine*, 66, pp. 162–76.

Gregory, Derek (1987) 'The Friction of Distance? Information Circulation and the Mails in Early Nineteenth-Century England', *Journal of Historical Geography*, 13, pp. 130–54.

Hadfield, Charles and Gordon Biddle (1970) *The Canals of the North-West of England*.

Haldane, A. R. B. (1952) *The Drove Roads of Scotland*. The most thorough study of droving, covering more than the title implies.

Harrison, A. E. (1985) 'The Origins and Growth of the U.K. Cycle Industry to 1900', *Journal of Transport History*, 3rd ser., VI, pp. 41–70.

Harrison, D. F. (1992) 'Bridges and Economic Development, 1300–1800', *Economic History Review*, 2nd ser., XLV, pp. 240–61.

Herbert, Nicholas (1985) *Road Travel and Transport in Gloucestershire*. Illustrates the quantity and range of information available from local newspapers.

Hey, David (1980) *Packmen, Carriers and Packhorse Roads: Trade and Communications in North Derbyshire and South Yorkshire*.

Hibbs, John (1989) *The History of British Bus Services* (2nd edn).

Hillman, Mayer and Anne Whalley (1979) *Walking IS Transport*.

Jackman, W. T. (1916) *The Development of Transportation in Modern England*. 2nd edition 1962 with introduction by W. H. Chaloner. For long the standard work, and still a major source of information, but now superseded in some of its judgements.

James, Francis (1975) *Walter Hancock and his Common Road Steam Carriages*.

Jenkins, J. Geraint (1961) *The English Farm Wagon: Origins and Structure*.

Jones, E. L. and M. E. Falkus (1979) 'Urban Improvement and the

English Economy in the Seventeenth and Eighteenth Centuries' in Paul Uselding (ed.), *Research in Economic History*, IV.

Klapper, Charles (1961) *The Golden Age of Tramways*.

Laux, James M. (1976) *In First Gear: The French Automobile Industry to 1914*.

Lewis, M. J. T. (1970) *Early Wooden Railways*.

Lewis, R. A. (1951) 'Transport for Eighteenth Century Ironworks', *Economica*, new ser., XVIII, pp. 278–84.

McKay, John P. (1976) *Tramways and Trolleys* (Princeton).

Mayhew, Henry (1967) *London Labour and the London Poor* (Cass edn).

Miller, John Anderson (1960) *Fares Please!* (New York).

Mingay, G. E. (ed.) (1989) *Agrarian History of England and Wales*, VI, *1750–1850*.

Morris, Arthur S. (1980) 'The Nineteenth Century Scottish Carrier Trade: Patterns of Decline', *Scottish Geographical Magazine*, 96, pp. 74–82.

Munby, D. L. (ed.) (1978) *Inland Transport Statistics: Great Britain, 1900–1970*, I.

Nicholson, T. R. (1982) *The Birth of the British Motor Car* (3 vols).

Owen, Nicholas (1974) *History of the British Trolley Bus*.

Pawson, Eric (1977) *Transport and Economy: The Turnpike Roads of Eighteenth Century Britain*.

Perren, Richard (1989) 'Markets and Marketing' in G. E. Mingay (ed.), *The Agrarian History of England and Wales*, VI, *1750–1850*, ch. VI especially 216–33 (Improvements in Transport) and 261–8 (Horses).

Plowden, William (1971) *The Motor Car and Politics, 1896–1970*.

Porter, Stephen (1982) 'Farm Transport in Huntingdonshire, 1610–1749', *Journal of Transport History*, III, pp. 35–45.

Pratt, Edwin A. (1912) *History of Inland Transport and Communication*.

Scola, Roger (1992) *Feeding the Victorian City. The Food Supply of Manchester, 1770–1870* (Manchester). An important pioneer study. Contains detailed information on the mode whereby each major foodstuff was brought to this rapidly growing northern city.

Simmons, Jack (1991) *The Victorian Railway*.

Smith, Donald J. (1985) *Horses at Work*.

Spufford, Margaret (1984) *The Great Reclothing of Rural England: Petty Chapmen and their Wares in the Seventeenth Century*.

Stern, Walter M. (1970) 'Fish Supplies for London in the 1760s: An Experiment in Overland Transport', *Journal of the Royal Society of Arts*, May and June, pp. 360–5, 430–5.

Sturt, George (1923) *The Wheelwright's Shop*.

Szostak, Rick (1991) *The Role of Transportation in the Industrial Revolution: a Comparison of England and France*. Gives full weight to road transport and its importance to the economy, though adding little new information about road services themselves.

Thompson, F. M. L. (1976) 'Nineteenth-Century Horse Sense', *Economic History Review*, 2nd ser., XXIX, pp. 60–81.

Trow-Smith, Robert (1959) *British Livestock Husbandry, 1700–1900.*

Tuck, Robert (1989) *Carrying Cargo: An Illustrated History of Road Haulage.* Concerns mechanised road haulage only.

Turnbull, Gerald L. (1977) 'Provincial Road Carrying in England in the Eighteenth Century', *Journal of Transport History*, 2nd ser., IV, pp. 17–39.

Turnbull, Gerald L. (1979) *Traffic and Transport: An Economic History of Pickfords.*

Turnbull, Gerald L. (1982) 'Scotch Linen, Storms, Wars and Privateers', *Journal of Transport History*, 3rd ser., III, pp. 47–69. The best analysis of the various influences on the transport decisions of a manufacturer.

Turnbull, Gerald L. (1985) 'State Regulation in the Eighteenth-Century English Economy: Another Look at Carriers' Rates', *Journal of Transport History*, 3rd ser., VI, pp. 18–36.

Vale, Edmund (1960) *The Mail-Coach Men of the late Eighteenth Century.*

Walker, Gilbert James (1942) *Road and Rail: An Enquiry into the Economics of Competition and State Control.*

Watson, W. Roderick and Martin Gray (1978) *The Penguin Book of the Bicycle.*

Webb, Sidney and Beatrice (1913) *The Story of the Kings Highway.*

Woodward, D. M. (1977) 'Cattle Droving in the Seventeenth Century: A Yorkshire Example', in W. H. Chaloner and Barrie M. Ratcliffe (eds), *Trade and Transport. Essays in Economic History in Honour of T. S. Willan* (Manchester). Based on valuable later seventeenth-century primary source material of the Warton family of Beverley.

Wrigley, E. A. (1962) 'The Supply of Raw Materials in the Industrial Revolution', *Economic History Review*, 2nd ser., XV, pp. 1–16.

Youatt, William (1831) *The Horse; with a Treatise on Draught.*

Index

New Studies in Economic and Social History

Previously published as

Studies in Economic History

Titles in the series available from the Macmillan Press Limited

Economic History Society

The Economic History Society, which numbers around 3,000 members, publishes the *Economic History Review* four times a year (free to members) and holds an annual conference.

Enquiries about membership should be addressed to

The Assistant Secretary
Economic History Society
PO Box 70
Kingswood
Bristol
BS15 5TB

Full-time students may join at special rates.